ABOUT THE AUTHOR

GUILLERMO QUINONEZ MD, MS, MA, FRCPC is a retired academic pathologist with forty years of practice and teaching in university hospitals. He is a former Professor of Pathology and Senior Scholar at the University of Manitoba, Canada. Dr Quinonez trained as a general pathologist at Ohio State University Hospitals and re-trained as an anatomic pathologist at McMaster University, Ontario, Canada, where he also did a fellowship in electron microscopy. He has an MS from Ohio State and MA in medical history from the Universities of Winnipeg and Manitoba. Dr Quinonez is an Emeritus Member of the Canadian Association of Pathologists/Association Canadienne des pathologists. He wrote this compendium as an Independent Scholar.

Tellwell Talent
www.tellwell.ca

ISBN
978-0-2288-7874-2 (Hardcover)
978-0-2288-7873-5 (Paperback)
978-0-2288-7875-9 (eBook)

WHAT IS ANATOMIC PATHOLOGY?

A Short History of a Medical Science

GUILLERMO QUINONEZ

Table of Contents

PREFACE

This is a compendium, NOT a textbook of anatomic pathology. It is the history of a medical science, i.e., AP, based on pathologic knowledge, knowledge that is common to all the sub-specialties of AP. Before my retirement in 2009, the idea to write a document to teach the basic reactions of the body to injury came to my mind. When years passed, I discovered that the topic could be expanded to include a context to this knowledge. At the very end, the compendium became a book on the history of knowledge in AP that explain what anatomical pathology represents for a pathologist.

When one finally retires, the connection to university libraries is lost. This is a problem because the source of literature is not readily available anymore. However, I have experienced that this is not an excuse. In this information age, the sources available in the internet are endless. Of them, I want to recognize two sources, "Wikipedia" and "Google Books." Of the first, I have taken the full name and date of birth and death of a substantial majority of savants and of the second have read several of the classics in the field that otherwise are not readily available when one does not have connection with a university library. In relation to sources, I should also mention the contribution of reprints and used books that are obtained at a reasonable cost. In synthesis, there are no excuses for retirees not to continue contributing to the literature.

Although this is not a book on social history, I would like to take the opportunity to thanks Professor James

Hanley of the University of Winnipeg, Manitoba, for introducing me to medical history. He also taught me not to write about contemporaneous events because someone, somewhere, will say that she/he was there and facts were not like that. His advice is respected in this book.

I would want to express gratitude to the opinion and support of former students of mine and several colleagues that reviewed parts or the whole original manuscript. The students are: Mauricio Lozano (El Salvador) (read part of Chapter 9 and Chapters 10, 13 and 14), Rafael Camacho (Spain) and Octavio Umaña (Canada) (read the whole manuscript). My colleagues are: Ricardo Padilla (Kaneda Distinguished Professor, University of North Carolina at Chapel Hill, USA) (read the whole manuscript), Noreen Walsh (Professor, Dalhousie University, Canada) (read the Epilogue), and Jacalyn Duffin (Professor Emerita, Queen's University, Canada) (read the Introduction, chapters 3, 4, 11, 12 and 15). Dr. Duffin made interesting observations that led me to reformulate the topic in order to make it more focused to the audience it was directed at. I modified the title as she suggested. Laurette Geldenhuys (Professor, Dalhousie University, Canada), by supporting my humanistic activities in the Canadian Association of Pathologists/association canadienne des pathologisties (2007-2016), influenced my interest on writing this book.

Guillermo Quinonez
Ontario, Canada, Spring of 2022.

INTRODUCTION

The history of anatomic pathology (AP) in the English-speaking countries of Great Britain, the United States, and Canada, is embedded in pathology textbooks and specialized medical history literature. On the one hand, the textbooks offer either short sections on such history or those aspects are embedded in the narrative. On the other hand, an extensive, specialized, and analytical literature consisting of books on medical history, book chapters, and journal articles certainly provides more focused historical information. This literature deals primarily with biographies, institutions, socio-political influences, culture, etc. and only secondarily with pathologic knowledge. Although crucial for having a broader perspective of the specialty and without denying its excellence, the author has not found in this literature a publication that specifically addresses the history of the 'foundational knowledge' of AP, essential to explain what is AP.

With this objective in mind, I have inverted the approach focusing primarily on pathologic knowledge and secondarily on biographies and institutions. The knowledge is the one utilized in practice and when training anatomic pathologists. The approach makes it possible to understand why anatomic pathologists use the biomedical model of disease; that is, the interpretation of disease from the point of view of the observer/experimenter (Satyarup et al. 2020, 8075-8079). It also explains how a pathologist view and think about her/his daily activities using valid knowledge obtained by the scientific method. In essence, the historical approach of the compendium would explain what AP is.

The history of the foundational pathologic knowledge (i.e., the basic reactions of the body to injury) is found in past and present pathology textbooks. Although dismissed by some because they do not present new discoveries, they undeniably provided contemporary learners with the "state-of-the-art" knowledge represented at a particular time (Kuhn 1996, xi; DeLanda 2015, xii). This knowledge is presented in statements that define it, concurrent with explanations that support the statements. The information is valid as descriptive and explanatory data (Zhang et al. 2004, 97-104).

Textbooks published in the British-North America literature can be organized into four historical periods: Emergence, Development, Consolidation, and Maturity. 'Emergence' extends from 1763, when Samuel Clossy (1724-1786) published the first textbook on AP in the English literature, to 1880 when books on the discipline appear in Britain-North America (Clossy 1763). During this period, there were few publications in English and the few popular textbooks were translations from French and German authors. The content of pathologic knowledge was found in textbooks on theoretical medicine called "Institutes of Medicine" (King 1982, 77); yet, some had no or minimal information about the topic (Paine [1847] 2009). Lack of publications is particularly noticeable in the third quarter of the nineteenth century when books on the subject produced by English authors were practically nonexistent (Long [1928] 1965). 'Development' extends from 1880 to 1920, the time around which bacteriology was also developing. Both disciplines grew together until around the end of WWI, in the 1920s, when each acquired their own identity and went their separate ways. 'Consolidation' spans from 1920 to 1960. In this period, biochemistry made great advances on understanding the cell's metabolism, and technical progress and professional changes occurred that impacted future developments. Technically, the introduction of electron microscopy and electrophoresis is worthy of mention. The knowledge generated set the basis for accelerated developments of the 'maturity' period (1960-1980). In this period, the practice of autopsies was neglected and, eventually, the attention moved to surgical- and cyto-pathology, which would become the main activity of general anatomic pathologists. The term 'maturity' refers here to a historical period and not to pathologic knowledge.

The foundational knowledge (i.e., the basic reactions of the body to injury) collected from these publications were called "Pathological Processes" by Rudolf Ludwig Carl Virchow (1821-1902) (Virchow [1860] 1978, ix, 279). It is a component of basic sciences, albeit it should not be equated with the entire content of the 'General Pathology' section of textbooks. The Pathological Processes are a common response of the body to different types of injury; i.e., independent of the type of injury, the reaction is similar. Examples of processes include inflammation, thrombosis, metaplasia, necrosis, neoplasia, fatty changes, degeneration, etc. Throughout the history of the specialty, they have achieved identity as a result of observation and experimentation under the context of morphology. They are essential for understanding the intimate mechanism of disease as discovered at autopsy and studied through nature and animal experiments. Without them, correct anatomoclinical correlation is impossible (Oertel 1927, 101). In 1980, the focus of pathological attention to study their nature changed to the 'cell' as the basic structure responsible for the reactions of the body to injury (Robbin and Cotran 1979).

The pathologic knowledge generated until 1980 was almost entirely based on the study of the phenotype; i.e., morphological appearances either macroscopic or microscopic. At that time, karyotyping was still preferred to study genetic diseases in man (Robbins and Cotran 1979, 213-218). But 1980 heralded the beginning of a new period (the contemporaneousness) in which the study of the genotype on a molecular level grew to prominence, hence the importance of this compendium if used as a historical baseline. In order to understand the evolution of knowledge is necessary, today and tomorrow, to understand the past, and this is my intention. The compendium was written around the phenotypical concept of morphology because AP is a morphological science and, although I believe that this fundamental idea will continue to prevail, I realize that it could change with future unforeseeable modifications. At the time of this writing, the impact of molecular pathology on AP as a morphological science; that is, molecular testing, is still preliminary. Will this discipline transform AP into a non-morphological science, or will it become another ancillary science as others before? Taking this into account, the history of the role of molecular pathology in AP, by whoever writes it today, most likely will be biased. There are already publications, but not enough time has elapsed to give a fair assessment of its impact on morphology (Vollmer and Goldmann 2011, 223-230; Mukherjee 2011, 2016).

****

The compendium is not a textbook of AP. It is about the history of pathologic knowledge and medical education (for health care students). Its content is divided in two parts. Part I titled "Background" comprises ten chapters. Its sources are 'classics' in the history of the specialty complemented with a selective review of the history literature. Chapter 1 is the history of the autopsy. Chapter 2 describes the evolution of the conceptualization of disease according to anatomic pathologists. In Chapter 3, what is understood as AP is evaluated; its division between basic and systemic; and the different uses of the term in the English world. Chapter 4 explains the significance of 'morphology' to this science. Chapter 5 covers the focus of attention (organs/tissue/cell) of the specialty followed in Chapter 6 by the history of the evolution of a method (the anatomoclinical), both developments necessary for the emergence of AP as a science. Chapter 7 describes the history of the first pathology atlases that illustrated gross anatomical lesions. In Chapter 8 there is an analysis of the knowledge's content of Virchow's *Cellular Pathology* – the beginnings of modern AP – followed in Chapter 9 with a review of the basic technology that has supported the growth of the specialty. Chapter 10 is a selected literature review of the history of the ancillary sciences to AP.

Part II is titled "Pathologic Knowledge" and consists of five chapters. Chapter 11 is an analysis of what is pathologic knowledge and its relation to scientific knowledge. Chapter 12 is an historical account of the basic reactions of the body to injury; that is, the "Pathological Processes." Chapter 13 and 14 contain the early history of two selected Processes. They are inflammation and neoplasia. Chapter 15 deals with an evaluation of pathologic knowledge to support the argument that this kind of knowledge is a variant of the scientific. Finally, there is an Epilogue in which I discuss the importance of the compendium in relation to the role that genetics would play in AP in the future. The compendium ends with a glossary and a bibliography.

PART I: BACKGROUND

CHAPTER 1

THE AUTOPSY

AP originated when the autopsy was introduced systematically to investigate the cause of death. Its contribution culminated with the development of a new concept in medicine, solidism, that replaced humouralism as an explanation of disease. Galen's humouralism, also known as "humourism", was an explanation that considers disease the result of an unbalance of four humours presents in the body. The humors were blood, yellow bile, black bile, and phlegm (mucus) (Perez-Tamayo 1961, 482, 483, 485). The history of the autopsy, and its relevance, is intertwined with that of anatomy, medicine, biology, and natural history (the corresponding old term for science). Based on the assumption that the autopsy is a technique, we have included reports from seminal works to illustrate the nature and application of its contribution and carefully selected information from the literature to add on its history. From such analysis, it is concluded that the knowledge obtained by the practice of autopsies created 'solidism', the concept that 'the site and cause' of clinical manifestations of disease is the body's organs. Solidism would provide the foundation for the anatomopathological conceptualization of disease.

1.1 *Practice of Autopsies*

Autopsies have been reported since antiquity. Since Greek times, it is well known that the physicians Herophilus (335-280 B.C.E.) and Erasistratus (c. 310-200 B.C.E.) practiced them in Alexandria (King and Meehan 1973, 514-544). In the early Middle Ages, between the fourth and the twelfth centuries, autopsies were performed in the Byzantine Empire, the Easter division of the Roman Empire whose capital was Constantinople, currently Istanbul, and the Western (Latin) division, whose capital was Rome. It has been reported that the Holy Roman Emperor Frederick II (1194-1250) signed a law the year 1231 authorizing the performance of human dissections (Finkbeiner et al. 2008, 3). Autopsies were practiced sporadically, not consistently, and sometimes not by physicians, with the intention to investigate the cause of death (Bliquez and Kazhdan 1984, 554-557; Browning 1985, 518-520; Carlino 1999, 151-152). Even done sporadically, such practice was prohibited in the world dominated by the Arabs because it was forbidden in the Koran (Finkbeiner et al. 2008, 2).

Historically, the Catholic Church was opposed to the practice of autopsies. There is evidence that one of the Fathers of the Church, Augustine (354-430), was against to such practice; unquestionably, the opposition was real. This antagonism slowly vanishes in the late Middle Ages, just before the beginnings of the Renaissance in the 1300s, as documented by autopsies performed on Popes and a bulla issued at that time (King and Meehan 1973, 514-544). It was Pope Honorius III (1150-1227) who indirectly gave impetus to the practice by prohibiting clergy to exercise medicine. Nevertheless, those who performed autopsies continued religious observance because the marvels of nature were considered God's work. Concomitantly, public health measures flourished, physicians organized in guilds, and hospitals were founded (Castiglioni 1941, 36-37).

Development of a more frequent practice of performing autopsies must be understood in the context of the evolution of thought brought about by the Renaissance. Before this intellectual era, Christian dogmas and Scholasticism dominated Western thought. The Renaissance challenged the status quo by going back to the Greeks. Among many, two aspects of the new thinking are important to consider. One was the notion that man is not the center of the universe, and the other was the Hellenistic concept that disease is an imbalance of nature and not God's punishment. Consequently, a cadaver was no longer considered something impure and a sacrilege to approach (Castiglioni 1941, 39-40, 54).

In medical education, the practice of autopsies was introduced in the curriculum after the 1300s. For instance, on May 7th, 1308, the Medical College at Venice was instructed by the Great Council of the city to "undertake one dissection a year" (Oertel 1927, 7-8). They were practiced in public and private houses with the intention to study normal anatomy and function (Park 1994). Galen's (129-c.210 C.E.) books provided the theoretical background of the curriculum; there was no questioning of his anatomical findings. At universities, the focus was shifted to anatomical theaters whose architecture has been immortalized in drawn paints (Snyder 2015, 238-239). The teacher sat in a kind of 'throne' where he read textbooks, in particular Galen's. Under him, the body was opened by assistants, commonly a barber-surgeon. Surrounding them was a gallery fill with students that observed the findings demonstrated by the assistants. Findings were not questioned. If they did not correspond to Galen's writings, they were ignored because 'Galen was always correct'.

At about the same time, autopsies began to be formally performed in Italy with the objective to investigate the cause of death, particularly in Bologna. The beginning is traced to this city in the first quarter of the fourteenth century. A professor at the University of Bologna, Mondino de Luzzi (c.1270-1326), wrote a textbook of anatomy in 1316 that included autopsy results (Osler [1913] 2009, 109). His interest in autopsies can be understood because that university was a center for the study of civil and canon law. Autopsies were performed having legal results in mind. Mundinus, as he was known, practiced public dissection with the intention of finding causes of death (Singer and Underwood 1962, 78, 80-81). Investigation of the cause of death was also the reason for performing autopsies during the epidemic of the Black plague that devastated the European population in 1348 (Park 1994, 1-33).

1.2 *"Anatomia Publica" and "Anatomia Privata"*

Two types of uses for autopsies, for teaching and for investigating the cause of death, created two kinds of practices, 'human dissection' for the first and 'post-mortem examination' for the second. At universities and anatomical theaters, human dissection was performed in bodies from healthy individuals most frequently obtained from hanged criminals and only rarely from hospitals (Cunningham 2010). *"Anatomia publica"* or "popular anatomy," as it was known, influenced medical education, but demonstrations were used only to observe size, colour, connections of organs, etc. and to correlate those findings with the humoral theory of disease according to Galen. Teaching of disease was theoretical (Klemperer 1958, 24-38). Nevertheless, the information was critically important for providing comparison of normal and diseased organs and their relationships. With no doubt, there had to be some questioning about approaching only the normal because abnormal findings had to be found in those bodies. Stated differently, human dissection for the purpose of medical education made possible observations and analogies that created a frame of mind that focused on anatomical findings as a critical component on the evolving knowledge about disease. For instance, the works of Mundinus' *Anatomy* and Andreas Vesalius' (1514-1564) *De Humani Corpora Fabrica*, both called attention to the importance of anatomical findings not only in the normal body but also in disease (Hannam 2011, 255-256).

Post-mortem examinations, on the other hand, were performed to investigate the cause of death in hospitalized patients (Sherrington 1946). It was known as *anatomia privata* (Klemperer 1958, 24-38). These examinations became the traditional technique to investigate disease in clinical practice. The post-mortems were not simply the satisfaction of a curiosity, but a curiosity that was scientifically based. P. Klemperer quotes Thomas Bartholin (1616-1689) on making the distinction between both types of practice in 1674 (Scarani 1994, 741-746). *'Anatomia privata'* differed from *'anatomia publica'* because its goal was anatomoclinical correlation; that is, the explanation of signs and symptoms given by lesions located at body organs (Cunningham, 1975). J. Fernel (1506-1558) had already expressed the difference and Marcello Malpighi (1628-1694) in the seventeenth century, stated, "… in autopsies one has to look for the sites and causes of diseases" (Scarani 1994, 741-746). Antonio Benivieni (1443-1502), Theophile Bonet (1620-1689), and G. B. Morgagni (1682-1771) practiced this type of anatomy between 1500 and the 1700s.

1.3 *Autopsy Reports in the Practice of "Anatomia Privata"*

Anatomy was normal and morbid since the beginnings of the practice of autopsies. Following the 1500s, practitioners of *'anatomia privata'* reported findings in the medical literature as brief statements. A publication that deserves particular attention is William Harvey's (1578-1657) *Lectures on the Whole of Anatomy*. He delivered the lectures as educational activities for surgeons at the Royal College of Physicians from 1615 to 1656 (Harvey [1616] 1961, 6). In them, Harvey stated his conceptualization of anatomy as, "observations of those things which occur rarely and as a morbid condition," and concludes that, "… dissection is useful for physicians; this more for surgeons for [relief of] the suffering" (22, 73). He made numerous references to autopsy findings in disease. For instance, "... In a dissection as far as the horns of the uterus I saw all the blood to have collected in the capacity of the abdomen through diabrosis [corrosion] (74). And, "... The Splen [sic] in cachetics or scorbutics [is] in some (not in all) very fully stuffed with blood so that [it is likely a] Bagg of blood" (104). Harvey was trained as an anatomist, and his interpretation of the lesions was based on humouralism. He made frequent references to Galen, Aristotle (384-322 B.C.E.), and Avicenna (c.980-1037) and mentioned comparative anatomy and occasional experimentation on cadavers (188). He personally performed autopsies, even one on his father (10).

Other publications offered more information on autopsy findings. For instance, Benivieni's *Hidden and Causes of Disease*, published in 1507, was organized by clinical cases in no particular order (Benivieni [1507] 1954). Very importantly, the reason for post-mortem examinations, with few exceptions, was to find the cause of death; consequently, examination of the body was not systematic. For instance, Case III stated, "Stones found in the coat of the liver" (25-27), was interpreted by him as the anatomical cause of death. Stones were gross and large and, therefore, easy to identify. Current anatomical knowledge would have influenced interpretation (Case LXXXIX) since the work was published 36 years before Vesalius' hallmark book on anatomy (169-171). There is no comparison (analogy) with or analyses of similar cases; and interpretation of observations is based on Galen (Case LXI) (127-129) and the humoural theory of disease (Case XXIX) (157-159). The importance of Benivieni's publication is the introduction of a systematized collection of autopsies by the first time (Krumbhaar [1937] 1962, 53).

In the seventeenth century, Bonet's *Sepulchretum siva anatomia practica* followed Benivieni's *Hidden and Causes of Disease*. It consisted of four books containing a collection of already published cases from the sixteenth and seventeenth centuries. It was organized by signs and symptoms but incorporated comments on autopsy findings, had a clinical rather than a pathological approach, and explanations were based on humouralism (Nicholls 1927, 463-466; Irons 1942, 623-665; Cunningham 2010, 193-194). The book was full of factual errors. After publication of the *Sepulchretum*, the Dutch authors Steven Blankaart (1650-1702) and Frederik Ruysch (1638-1731) published similar collections of cases (Krumbhaar [1937] 1962, 57).

In the eighteenth century, two hundred fifty years after Benivieni's publication, in 1756, Albert Haller (1708-1777) published *Pathological Observations, Chiefly from Dissections of Morbid Bodies* (Haller 1756). This work may have not received the attention it deserves. Haller's observations did not include a whole discussion of the case but emphasized the anatomical findings. The book consists of sixty-two pathological observations, which included animal cases, that were mostly classified anatomically. The descriptions are detailed but limited to the organ that showed the morbid changes. For instance, in Observation No. 4, corresponding to a case of an aneurism of the carotid artery, he wrote, "Death delivered the patient from the dangerous operation, ... There being no time to lose, we dissected the affected parts that evening. The skin being removed, the tumour itself came immediately in view, and was membraneous, cellular, spongy, adhering to the skin, and more than twice as large as one's fist. ..." (7). He also combined observations at autopsy with living animal experimentation. In Observation XXVII, a case of intususception of the intestines in which he did not demonstrate inflammation, Haller reproduced the lesion in a rabbit and in frogs to confirm the lack of inflammation (53). In other observations, he compared findings with that of an elephant: "... as in the bile of the elephant nothing seems wanting, although this animal has no gall-bladder" (92). Haller used Galen's humoral theory, and explanations were designed to prove his point of view. Adding to Haller's systematic investigations of autopsies with its emphasis on anatomy, Joseph Lieutaud's (1703-1780) *Historia Anatomica-medica*, published a collection of 1200 autopsies organized by organs rather than by symptoms. In spite of this abundant literature, none had fulfilled the degree of systematization introduced by Morgagni (Krumbhaar [1937] 1962, 58).

In comparison to Haller and about the same time, G.B. Morgagni published in 1761 *Seats and Causes of Disease* (Morgagni [1769] 1983). This book had a more extensive and comprehensive description of autopsy findings than any publications at that time and was written in an epistolary style. In it, Morgagni defended the practice of autopsies, by saying, "... in which I might demonstrate how great an advantage there is arising from the dissections of dead bodies" (xxviii). However, anatomical findings are only complementary to other clinical data. In contrast to Benivieni's descriptions, Morgagni's autopsy lesions are compared with normal anatomical appearance during a time when anatomy was well developed as a discipline (Letter fourth). Descriptions are of various lengths and detailed, but in general lesions are systematically described. They also include crude chemical texts (mixture of body secretions with chemical reagents) (Letter fourth), animal experimentation (vivisection) (Letter fifty-nine), legal medicine (hanging) (Letter nineteenth), and oncological surgical pathology (gross examination of removed tumors) (Letter fifty). The intention was the explanation of symptoms by autopsy findings (Letter twenty). For this reason, anatomic descriptions are comprehensive. For instance, in a case "Of tumor and pain in the hypochondria", he said, "The abdomen was found full of a yellow water, which was bitter in its taste, and, like the serum of the blood, coagulated when on the fire. ..." (Letter eight). He continues describing findings in the abdomen and thorax and comparing them with previous cases. He then refers to his experience with the nature of the abdominal fluid found at autopsy in liver's cysts (hydatids) and the drain of liver abscesses to the intestines via the biliary ducts. Interestingly, the head is usually not included in the reports because there were no symptoms related to that anatomical space that indicated the need to dissect it. He uses Galen in some of his explanations, but the idea that the sites and causes of disease was represented in the body's organs was fully developed. Morgagni also described conditions under which autopsies were performed. Dissections lasted for several days (Letter fifty-third), usually performed at the hospital (Letter fifty-fifth), junior members of the staff executed many of them

(Letter fifty-fifth), and there were assistants helping the main dissector. Some autopsies were limited depending on the questions arising during the life of the patient or due to lack of preservation of the body since there were no fixatives (Letter third). The head was separated from the body first; conditions of putrefaction varied based on the time of the year, that is, winter vs. summer; dissections sometimes were stopped due to bad smelling (Letter fifty-fourth). Autopsies were frequently problem oriented and limited to certain body's areas based on symptoms, but in some other cases they were complete. Teaching added annual demonstrations in wintertime (Letter fifty-third).

In 1763, two years after Morgagni's publication, Samuel Clossy's (c. 1724-1786), *Observations On some of the Diseases Of the Parts of the Human Body: Chiefly taken from the Dissections of Morbid Bodies* was published in Great Britain (Clossy [1763] 1967). The *Observations* is organized by clinical cases. There are fifty-three cases distributed by body region and organs: head, neck & chest, liver, dropsy, intestines, kidneys, and urinary bladder. The only exception is 'dropsy'. Each case is titled by its symptom. In general, pathogenesis is explained by the assumption that organs are made of fibers (71-72). Trial and experience were his approach for recognizing the limitation of autopsies in anatomoclinical correlation (81). The publications by Morgagni, Clossy, and Haller, working independently, indicate that the style to use anatomoclinical correlation based on changes in the human body's organs observed at the autopsy was well established in Europe at the middle of the eighteenth century (Quinonez and Geldenhuys 2019).

1.4 *Consequences*

A consequence of the systematic practice of autopsies was the introduction of solidism, a concept that eventually would replace humouralism. Solidism was understood in relation with the concurrent structural conception of the body that considered it built by solids, fluids, and a vital principle or soul that controlled the other two. In a sense, humouralism was based on the body's fluids whereas solidism recognized the importance of the location of disease in organs as was well presented in Morgagni's work. However, it also raised the question of causality. Is the lesion present at autopsy not only the site of the disease but also the cause of the clinical manifestations? The location was easily assumed, but the question about causality persisted for the following century until the development of the germ-theory of disease and the Koch's postulates. In the first half of the nineteenth century, the autopsy became the tool of the Paris and the New Vienna Schools. In the decades that followed, it continued playing a crucial role on the development of knowledge in AP as illustrated in its importance for completing the study of disease promoted by William Osler (1849-1919) (Rodin 1981). It is at the middle of the twentieth century that the practice of autopsies entered into crisis due to economic reasons (who pay for it?) and advances in diagnostic imaging, among others.

1.5 *Conclusions*

The practice of autopsies as *"anatomia privata"* was slowly but firmly incorporated into the practice of academic medicine from the sixteenth to middle of the eighteenth century. It is evident that anatomy was morbid since its very beginnings. Initially, autopsy results were used to investigate the cause of death, and the morbid descriptions became only supplementary to clinical information. Although Galen's humouralism was frequently used for interpretation of findings, a new 'focus of attention' away from fluids was developing. Physicians began to recognize that focusing on morbid findings (observation) and comparing them to normal organs (analogy) could be used independently of humouralism to explain signs and symptoms of disease. Consequently, a modification of thinking resulted in a new concept called solidism, a concept that became the basis for a new conceptualization of disease, the anatomoclinical. This fundamental change in the interpretation of disease brought far-reaching implications. From the idea of solidism derives a focus of attention (the body's organs) and a method (the anatomoclinical), both minimal criteria for the origin of AP as a new science.

CHAPTER 2

THE NATURE
OF DISEASE

In the course of human history, theories about the nature of disease appear to follow the three evolutionary stages of human knowledge described by Comte in his positivist philosophy (Martineau 1875, 358-360; Temkin 1977, 419-449). They are: theological, metaphysical, and positive (Martineau 1875). By 'nature' I understand the structural and functional changes produced in the body by a disease and its manifestation as signs and symptoms. In the 'theological stage', gods and natural phenomena explain events as they are perceived (Martineau 2875, 2). The humoural theory of disease is an example of a theory in the 'metaphysical stage' (Porter 2002, 25-30). It persisted until the middle of the nineteenth century as illustrated by the neo-humouralism of Carl von Rokitansky (1804-1878) who conjectured that an imbalance of fibrin and albumin in the blood was the cause of disease (Rokitansky 1854; Porter 1997, 330-331). In the 'positive stage', knowledge is scientific and acquired by observation and reasoning using the scientific method (Martineau 1875, 1-2). This is the stage relevant to the modern conception of the nature of disease.

Other postulated theories were of short duration and disappeared due to lack of evidence. Those by Herman Boerhaave (1668-1738) and the Systematists are good examples. The first considered disease a static event (Hess n.d., 13-14), and the second, proposed by Georg Ernst Stahl (1659-1734), William Cullen (1710-1790) and John Brown (1735-1788), postulated systems based on the contraction and relaxation of the body's solids (Krumbhaar [1937] 1962, 30-32, 34). It is when these theories were popular that an anatomopathological conception was introduced.

The anatomopathological conception, evolving since the Renaissance, was still not accepted at the end of the eighteenth century when classificatory systems were still debated (Rymer 1775, xi; Foucault 1994, 4). Experimental support was lacking. AP had no impact on the practice of medicine and, conversely, on the understanding of disease. It is under these conditions that Morgagni, in 1761, solidified the evolving idea of solidism by correlating clinical signs and symptoms with autopsy findings; that is, an anatomopathological understanding of disease. However, his attempt was not popular in the rest of the eighteenth century. It had to wait until the nineteenth when the Paris School of medicine began to practice this new conceptualization (Ackernetch 1967).

Yet, the new conception had limitations. Some signs and symptoms had no anatomical explanation at autopsy, and only some of the basic reactions of the body to injury - the foundational knowledge of AP - had been described but were not yet systematized. These were the conditions at the middle of the nineteenth century when, using the scientific method, Virchow modified the anatomopathological conception by introducing cellular pathology. After Virchow's work, the concept evolved within positivism and concluded with considering it as a deviated state from health (Virchow [1847] 1971, 233).

For anatomic pathologists, the conceptualization of disease has certain particularities that need to be considered as found in selected textbooks of pathology published in the four periods of the history of knowledge in AP. The four periods are: Emergence (before 1880), Development (1880-1920), Consolidation (1920-1960), and Maturity (1960-1980).

2.1 *Emergence (1763-1880)*

In the first textbook of pathology published in Great Britain in 1763, *Observations On some of the Diseases Of the Parts of the Human Body: Chiefly taken from the Dissections of Morbid Bodies*, Samuel Clossy considered that the organic lesion or its functional expression is the disease (Clossy [1763] 1967, v). No different from Morgagni's and John Hunter's (1728-1793) conclusion, the lesion was the site and cause of disease (Morgagni [1769] 1983, 189). Anything could produce an organic lesion, and the symptom was a preternatural expression of the disease (Clossy [1763] 1967, v).

William Horner (1793-1853), in his *A Treatise on Pathological Anatomy* published in America 66 years later in 1829, maintained the same explanation (Quinonez and Maclendon 2011). Disease was not an ontological entity; that is, it did not have an independent existence.

According to him, the ontological concept represented the end of the medical theories so popular in those years. Disease is located in organs, and the organic lesion is the disease (Horner 1829, x). The anatomical lesions manifest as alterations of organs in form, size, and texture (10). He considered that diseases without anatomical findings at autopsy were 'nervous' in origin (xiii). In relation to causality, any physical agent (i.e., air, water, heat, electricity, food, etc.) could predispose or cause diseases, providing that they were applied to susceptible individuals either in excessive or insufficient amounts. Susceptibility was determined by life's habits, and factors such as, age, sex, heredity, and temperaments, the latter a remnant of humouralism (9). Horner's opinion on disease as a non-ontological entity is supported by historians today as a common opinion in North America in those years (Rosenberg 1987, 73). However, a different view began to emerge at the middle of the nineteenth century.

When Samuel David Gross (1805-1884) published the third edition of his *Elements of Pathological Anatomy* in the U.S. in 1856, a veiled statement appeared indicating that disease could be seen as an alteration of health. The alteration would consist of a modification of the function or structure in the healthy body (Gross 1857, 36). Yet, there was still a dominant component of previous interpretations. He classified diseases into functional and organic. Functional would be equivalent to Horner's 'nervous' while organic corresponds to an alteration of textures, that is, tissues (36). However, there were doubts at the time. Gross admitted that the nature of disease was unknown and that more research needed to be done in the pathology of the vascular and nervous system in order to understand its nature (36). The reason for this statement had to be the neo-humouralistic view during the middle of the nineteenth century that causality of disease was an alteration of the blood that affects the tissues, a statement strongly supported in a contemporary text, Rokitansky's *A Manual of Pathological Anatomy* (Rokitansky 1854). In any case, Gross' opinion represented the beginning of change.

Simultaneously, Virchow's established a principle that revolutionized our understanding and eliminated humoral explanations. The principle states that physiology and pathology should be explained by studying the cell's mechanisms resulting from environmental influences. The principle incorporated cause and effect in the explanation. Consequently, a new stage in the history of disease relevant to pathology dawned, resulting in an abandonment of theories based on speculation and partial facts and support for materialistic explanations that could be explored experimentally. The new cellular pathology would explain the nature of disease by demonstrating the basic reaction of the body to injury morphologically and extrapolating those findings to function (Oertel 1927, 15-17). Publications appearing in the last quarter of the nineteenth century offered the new interpretation initiated by Virchow.

2.2 Development (1880-1920)

The new conception was already accepted in the literature by 1881. T. Henry Green states in *An*

Introduction to Pathology and Morbid Anatomy that disease is a deviation from health and that deviation corresponds to changes in the structure and function of tissues and organs. In disease, the human body does not perform as in health. Although still classifying diseases into organic and functional, he suggested that the latter may have been due to ignorance because the number of diseases classified as functional decreased with the introduction of the light microscope. Health and disease, therefore, became relative terms that cannot be treated independently and have no well-defined boundary. As he stated, "They are expressions of life" (Green 1881, 17-18). In 1889, D. J. Hamilton, in *A Text-Book of Pathology*, exemplified the changes in structure and function by explaining that an abnormal number of renal glomeruli is an example of a structural disease, whereas an increase of certain substances or the appearance of new ones in the glomeruli's filtrate indicates functional disease (Hamilton 1889, 162).

At the beginnings of the twentieth century, Green and Hamilton's statements were improved. Francis Delafield (1841-1915) and Theophil Mitchell Prudden (1849-1924), in their book published in 1901, *A Handbook of Pathological Anatomy and Histology*, emphasized that disease was not an entity but a process caused by internal and external agents. They stressed that disease was to a greater extent a functional alteration of the body that may or may not be accompanied by structural changes (Delafield and Prudden 1901, 65, 166). J. George Adami (1862-1926) in his *The Principles of Pathology*, published in 1908, is more specific on the meaning of 'functional'. He considered this term synonymous with 'metabolism', and maintained that there was a metabolic equilibrium in a healthy state that was lost in disease. For him, Pathological Processes were examples of an altered physiology, and from that, he supported the importance of physiology in AP (Adami 1908, 20-21).

William Thomas Councilman (1854-1933), in his book *Pathology* published in 1912, stressed the role of the environment in causality. Evidently, this was consequence of the emergency of bacteriology because he mentions the importance of the agent (i.e., micro-organisms) and the necessity of incorporate it in the investigation of lesions. He also mentioned the need to extend these investigations with microscopical and chemical studies (Councilman 1912, 17-19). Finally, Guthrie McConnell, in *A Manual of Pathology* published in 1915, emphasized that disease was a structural and functional deviation from the normal (McConnell 1915, 17). These points simply expanded on the explanatory principle introduced by Virchow.

2.3 *Consolidation (1920-1960)*

During the rest of the twentieth century, the understanding of the nature of disease was elaborated as an entity around Virchow's principle; namely, physiology (health) and pathology (disease) should be explained by studying the cell's mechanisms resulting from environmental influences. Oertel (1871-1956) in his book *Outlines of Pathology* published in 1927, made a passionate argument around the conceptualization based on cellular pathology (Oertel 1927). For him, the term 'cellular pathology' was misleading because it does not refer to cells only, but incorporates tissues and organs, which are the basis to explain the nature of disease. Such findings offer clinicians the elements to make diagnoses and treat patients (18-22). For this author, disease was a subjective name given to body lesions; it was the object and not the subject of inquiry. The role of the anatomical pathologist was to give a scientific explanation for the manifestations of the disease; that is, etiopathogenesis (mechanism) and anatomoclinical correlation. His role was not to diagnose, this was the responsibility of the clinician (159). Years later and in the same vein, William Boyd (1885-1979) reiterated in *A Text-Book of Pathology* that disease is not a state but a process resulting from a summation of abnormal chemical reactions; that is, metabolism (Boyd 1938, 16).

2.4 *Maturity (1960-1980)*

In the middle of the twentieth century, D. F. Cappell wrote a summary of the current understanding of disease in Muir's *Textbook of Pathology* (Cappell 1964). It is now unquestionably accepted that an alteration of health is caused by the biochemical body's reactions. Morphological changes not always follow these alterations. In the case of an infection, the cause must act under proper circumstances in a susceptible individual. For the first time, genetic disorders were introduced to causality (xi-xii). In general, for disease to occur there must be a cause and a reaction in the body of the affected individual. That is, disease is the consequence of such interaction (v); it does not have existence by itself. In that interaction, changes in structure are followed by functional disorders (ix). Finally, W.A.D. Anderson (1910-1986), in *Pathology*, demanded that any knowledge about the nature of disease belongs to pathology (Anderson 1971). It is in AP that any knowledge generated in other areas, like genetics, cytology, biochemistry, clinical sciences, etc., must be summarized. Although pathologists frequently stress morphology over function, Anderson undeniably considered that anatomy and histology continue being, to that date (i.e., the 1970's), "the essential foundation of knowledge about diseases;" that is, its nature (x).

2.5 Corollary

This review supports the evidence that the anatomopathological conceptualization of the nature disease is the one used by anatomic pathologists since Virchow's times up to 1980. It has evolved according to the partial contribution of AP to the whole idea of disease in medicine. In the general classification of concepts (models) of disease, it corresponds to the 'biomedical'; that is, the interpretation of disease from the point of view of the observer/experimenter, in this case, the pathologist. The anatomopathological concept is equivalent to the clinicopathological model of disease used by clinicians every day.

The anatomopathological concept is explicable by the production and acquisition of knowledge in the practice of pathology. Matters of fact, with few exceptions, are obtained not at bed-side but in offices under the microscope, in autopsy rooms, on laboratory benches, and are discussed in conference rooms. This scenario is an individualistic practice, albeit does not exclude incorporation of external factors in disease.

2.6 Conclusions

The history of the 'nature' of disease in Britain-North America has two stages, before and after Virchow. Before Virchow, the lesion was considered the site and cause of disease and the whole explanation had features of humouralism. It was named the "anatomopathological" conception by the French, but it had limitations. Some signs and symptoms had no anatomical explanation at autopsy; only some of the reactions of the body to injury had been described; and the reactions were not systematized. After Virchow, the anatomopathological concept evolved in accordance with his idea of "cellular pathology" with positivism as the approach, and, as found in the pathology literature, considering the nature of disease a deviated state from health at the cellular level. The evolution would address the original limitations. Explanations of signs and symptoms at autopsy were more frequently found due to new knowledge generated by experimentation and technology, the contributions of the ancillary sciences, and the role of the environment. The reactions of the body to injury were properly identified and new ones added as a result of the application of the scientific method. Once thoroughly identified, the reactions were systematized and used for explaining signs and symptoms. Using the new knowledge, it became evident that disease is the expression of an alteration of health, that is, of normal mechanisms. The anatomopathological conceptualization, therefore, evolved to recognize that is not the complete explanation of disease but only of its 'nature' as a deviated state from health.

This was the conception of the nature of disease in AP up to 1980. Let's not forget, however, that in the future a complete explanation might incorporate genetics and that a complete account in medicine should include socio-cultural-economic factors.

CHAPTER 3

THE SIGNIFICATION OF THE TERM "ANATOMIC PATHOLOGY"

The terms AP and 'pathology' are frequently used interchangeably, although they are not synonymous. Making the distinction is important for uncover the meaning of AP. The etymology of the term pathology is 'the study of disease' in general, whereas AP is the branch of pathology that studies only some aspects of disease. As a branch of anatomy, AP inherited from this science its morphological origin, and as a morphological science is no different from embryology, histology, radiology, neuropathology, etc. In this and the following chapter, we are clarifying the confusion of the terminology and the lack of reflection about the connotation of the term 'morphology' in this context by exploring 'the signification of the term AP' and by explaining 'what is morphology'.

Using the traditional requirement of a science, pathology is a pure, factual, empirical discipline consequently applicable to an applied science, that is, medicine (Klemke et al. 1998, 29-34). Pathology is the study of disease and an umbrella term for several sub-specialties of which AP is one of them. Some may argue that the distinction between pathology and AP is only a matter of terminology. This statement was true a century ago when pathology was the same as 'morbid anatomy' (Cappell 1964, v-vi). Consequently, the distinction today is historically relevant because pathology has expanded to include other kinds of knowledge, whereas morbid anatomy has become AP and has been maintained as its morphological branch. Morphology is the foundation of its identity, something that cannot be said of pathology in general. Being a well-defined science, the significance of AP can be obtained from the classification, usage, and definition of the term 'pathology'. An additional understanding is obtained from the consideration that AP is a system of knowledge.

3.1 *Classification and Usage of the Term 'Pathology'*

The classification and usage of the term 'pathology' in North America is well recognized professionally. At hospitals, pathology is divided into 'anatomical' and 'clinical', an administrative division that corresponds to specific needs. Clinical pathology is subdivided into sub-specialties independent from the anatomical division, such as hematopathology, clinical chemistry, and microbiology. AP, the morphological component, is subdivided into autopsy, surgical pathology, and cytopathology. Each of these subdivisions has several subspecialties that reflect both technological developments and societal needs. Autopsy pathology is the post-mortem examination of bodies to determine the cause of death and to explain the mechanisms of disease in the living body. It has evolved as quality control for medical practice. Closely associated is forensic pathology, the scientific contribution of the autopsy to medico-legal investigations. Surgical pathology is the study of specimens resected by surgeons and cytopathology is the examination of cells, both for diagnostic purposes. To them, one can add those applications of AP to specific body systems, such as neuropathology, nephro-pathology, gyne-pathology, etc. This North American hospital classification, however, changes across the Atlantic.

In the United Kingdom, the use of the term 'pathology' at hospitals is different and utilitarian. The term 'clinical pathology' is used when referring to the practice of examining body tissue and fluids for diagnostic purposes (Foster 1959, 173-187); that is, it includes both North American divisions (anatomic and clinical) as practiced in a hospital setting.

In the pathology literature of Great Britain and North America, the term 'pathology' refers to AP. Textbooks are books of AP organized into 'General' and 'Systemic' sections. General Pathology, also called 'Basic Science Pathology', is the common denominator to all branches of AP (Oertel 1927, 26). The term 'basic sciences' is applied to the disciplines of biology, chemistry, physics, and mathematics. In medicine, the experimental (laboratory) component of pathology is considered a basic science. In the textbooks, basic science is made of two components: (1) the body's reactions to injury, the foundational knowledge of the science, and (2) the sciences that are ancillary to the specialty, such as bacteriology, immunology, genetics, parasitology, and so forth. As here addressed, basic science does not refer to the whole content of the section, but specifically to the study of the reactions of the body to injury; namely, the Pathological Processes. The Systemic Pathology section covers the application of basic science to the diseases of the body's systems.

A new term that could appear as an alternative to the division of pathology into basic and clinical is 'Translational Science' or research. The term, as defined by the "European Society for Translational Medicine" refers to the immediate application of results obtained from laboratory (basic) research, clinical studies, and population studies (Cohrs et al. 2015, 86-88).

As noted, classifications and usages of the term 'pathology' are varied which may explain its loose meanings in health care and beyond. The various uses also illustrate the complexity of the field, and are the likely reasons for the confusion for the uninitiated when distinguishing it from AP.

3.2 *The Definition of 'Anatomic Pathology'*

The meaning of the term 'pathology' follows its etymology, that is, 'the study of disease'. For instance, in the Merriam-Webster's Medical Desk Dictionary, pathology is defined as, "the study of the essential nature of diseases and esp [sic] of the structural and functional changes produced by them." Similar definitions are given in other medical dictionaries and in pathology books (Adami 1908, 23; Cappell 1964, v). Long's classical textbook of the history of pathology states that, "pathology deals with the fundamental nature of disease" (Long [1928] 1965, 3). These short earlier definitions contrast with the descriptive and comprehensive one introduced by Malkin who wrote in 1993 that 'pathology' is 'that branch of natural science that studies the cause and mechanism of disease and includes: (1) structural changes in the cells, tissues, and organs, both gross and microscopic; (2) disturbances of function at the cell, tissue, or organ level; (3) the relationship of the signs and symptoms of the patient to both the structural and functional abnormalities; (4) methods used to detect both structural and functional abnormalities; and (5) identification of external and internal factors initiating structural or functional changes" (Malkin 1993, 8). Malkin's definition is a definition of AP because it "studies the cause and mechanisms of disease."

Disease, as a concept, consists of etiology, epidemiology, ecology, signs and symptoms, diagnosis, pathogenesis, prognosis, treatment, etc. 'Morphological expert knowledge' draws conclusions about only 'certain' of these aspects. AP participates partially because the conceptualization of disease is extensive enough to depend solely on morphological explanations. Morphology is used to study causality, pathogenesis (mechanism), and anatomoclinical correlation (Quinonez 2010, 13-18). Support for this statement is based on the fact that disease can be defined at various levels, and morphology is only one of them. For instance, SNOMED (Systematized Nomenclature of Medicine) considered that disease can be defined from several points of view, such as pathological findings (e.g., basal cell carcinoma), symptoms presentation (e.g., skin allergy), etiology (e.g., typhoid fever), etc. (Gantner et al. 1979, 22).

3.3 *Anatomic Pathology as a 'System of Knowledge'*

Jacalyn Duffin has introduced an understanding of 'pathology' that can be applied to AP. She states that 'pathology' is, "a system of knowledge used to draw conclusions about illness. ... validated by current science and philosophy" (Duffin 2010, 65). 'System of knowledge' has been interpreted also as "an analyzable body of knowledge" (Moulin 1989, 294). However, Duffin's interpretation of a 'system of knowledge' is more comprehensive. Her explanation calls attention to three conditions: a 'system of knowledge', 'current science', and 'philosophy'. Since this explanation is generic and, being AP a branch of pathology, it is also applicable to this science. Therefore, I can paraphrase that AP is also a system of knowledge because pathologic knowledge is used to draw conclusions about certain manifestations of disease. The system (the procedures to obtain it, the scientific method) is validated by its scientific content (the corpus of knowledge) and by a philosophy (positivism, the context). Duffin's understanding offers the opportunity of using the elements of her interpretation as a guide to write the history of AP.

3.4 *Conclusions*

AP is the morphological branch of 'pathology' *par excellence*. It is not simply a technique, but a scientific discipline. Its aim is to identify and explain the etiopathogenesis of disease using structural manifestations in the body and their clinical expressions. An understanding of AP as a system of knowledge would offer also the elements to design avenues to write history from other perspectives. These considerations answer the question about the signification of the term AP. It is unlikely that this understanding will be affected by further scientific advances, such as molecular pathology and artificial intelligence, among others. The terminology could be modified but, unless these developments transform AP from a morphological to a non-morphological science, its identity will be preserved.

CHAPTER 4

WHAT IS MORPHOLOGY

Morphology is the essence of AP. In this science, the term morphology has two meanings, as a 'description' and as a 'mental representation'. As a description, morphology is understood as the configuration, shape, or particular appearance of body's organs, tissues, and cells; and, for our purpose, it is equated with phenotype (Oertel 1927, 155). In this context, the term is applied to the evaluation of images obtained from specimens studied grossly and microscopically. The description is particular and universal at the same time; meaning that pattern descriptions are applicable to a particular observation but also to any others of the same class in future observations. When morphology is applied as a descriptor to future observations, it eventually becomes a mental representation in the memory of the pathologist; that is, as knowledge stored in long-term memory in the form of discourse and images (Westerhoff 2011, 77-80). These representations are formed through teaching/learning (i.e., education), improved by practice and experience, and influenced by the opinion of a community of anatomic pathologists.

The origin of morphology in science dates back to antiquity, but the first attempts to study the body's form - as we know it today – goes back to the late Middle Ages for forensic reasons; to the Renaissance with the works of the master painters of the human form, like Leonardo and Michelangelo; and to the introduction of the autopsy. It was in these years that authors began to explain disease based on observed organic changes (that is, morphology) rather than on humouralism, the dominant theory at that time. The investigation was later expanded to tissues and cells. Morphology, therefore, was directed to discover the characteristics of the body's compartments (i.e., organ, tissue, cell) and to explain the mechanism of their diseases. The end result was the transformation from describing the particular morphological attributes of a lifeless form to explaining the vital reactions of the body to injury.

4.1 *Evaluation of Morphology as a Manifestation of a Historical Process*

The observation of the morphology of the body's compartments progressed from macro- to micro-structures. New technology, observation, experimentation, and advances in knowledge contributed to more precision in interpreting morphology for AP. Such interpretation has been the result of the progressive introduction of evaluation of the three compartments of the body: organ, tissue, and cells; although the compartments are not necessarily evaluated in this sequence in a particular case today. Initially, the study of 'organs' intermingled with the practice of autopsies. This was followed by the study of 'tissues' with the introduction of microscopy. It was a contribution of histology and does not correspond to the concept of tissue promoted by Bichat. The final progression was the introduction of the 'cell' by Virchow. The study of the cell began with the appraisal of the cytoplasm about one full century before the study of the nuclear content (i.e., genetic material) was introduced.

The morphology of the body's compartments (organ/tissue/cell) has facilitated the assessment of structure and function in an integrated manner. Mayr has called it "explanatory reductionism", and it is of great didactic utility (Mayr 1982, 60-62, 64-66; Klee 1997, 81-102; Westerhoff 2011, 34, 48-49). Each compartment represents an increment/decrement in complexity, complexity referring to the perceptual process required for interpretation. Between compartments, fuzzy demarcation is the norm rather than the exception. The evaluation of one compartment does not exclude the other, but explains it; and the explanation must not be interpreted as reducing and/or eliminating another. The object of study can be systematically divided for the purpose of analysis if proceeding downwards on the compartments (organ/tissue/cell), or proceeding upwards for the purpose of synthesis (cell/tissue/organ).

In AP, each compartment has its own methodology for study. The organ is studied by gross observation; the tissue and the cell by light microscopy, histochemistry, electron microscopy, immunohisto(cyto)chemistry, and molecular morphology. Consequently, each compartment has generated new sub-specialties. For instance, organs are the basis of medical autopsy and forensic pathology; tissues the basis of histopathology; cells the basis of cytopathology, and molecular morphology the basis of molecular pathology.

Pathologists study the compartments as the source of morphological data to generate expert knowledge. They analyze structural and functional phenotypes in organ/tissue/cell with the naked eye and technological devices. Structural phenotypes are observed tri-dimensionally during gross examination or bi-dimensionally under the microscope. The bi-dimensional is expressed as architectural arrangements (tissue patterns) and characteristic cell morphology (cell patterns). On the other hand, functional phenotypes are expressed by distorted secretory or mitotic activity, antigenic constitution, or by the cell's genetic material. The distorted secretory activity is observed by histochemistry, immunohistochemistry, and electron microscopy; the antigenic constitution of the cells' antigenic receptors is evaluated by immunohisto(cyto)chemistry; whereas the genetic material is studied by molecular pathology techniques. From this morphological analysis, pathologists create gross and microscopic descriptions and infer pathologic (expert) knowledge.

4.2 Conclusions

Morphology in AP has two connotations, as a description and as knowledge stored in long-term memory. The description has evolved historically and is obtained by a process of perception of the body's compartments (organ, tissue, cell). The process takes advantage of the hierarchical structure of nature, with or without technological aids. Such knowledge becomes stored in the long-term memory of anatomic pathologists. I consider morphology, therefore, the codification of a perceived descriptive and explanatory regularity in nature that becomes a learned representation of form and its meaning.

By the end of the twentieth century, morphology had produced the largest body of knowledge in AP. This statement does not mean that morphology no longer useful, but it has become necessary to look for other avenues to improve detection of its manifestations (Quinonez 2002). This is happening by extending the evaluation of cells to their genetic material, as studied by molecular pathology. It appears that Virchow's cellular pathology is here to stay.

CHAPTER 5

THE FOCUS OF ATTENTION: ORGAN/ TISSUE/CELL

The history of the origin of AP is found in medical books published between the early 1500s and the middle 1700s. These treatises are recognized by their content on autopsy reports and their respective anatomoclinical correlations. Benivieni's *De Abditis Nonnullis Ac Mirandis Morborum et Sanationum Causis* was the first document of a quasi-systematic practice of autopsies for the purpose of investigating the cause of death and his publication coincided with the beginnings of modern science, at the Renaissance. A series of publications in the next two and a half centuries followed, demonstrating the importance of recognizing the body's organs as the site of damage in disease and the correlation of these findings with manifested signs and symptoms. It became evident that these results provided a better model to explain disease than the one by Galen's humouralism. At the middle of the 1700s, Morgagni's *Seats and Causes of Disease* re-capitulated this accumulated knowledge, setting the minimal conditions for the origin of AP as a science; namely, by identifying the "focus of attention" (i.e., the body's organs) and the "method" of investigation (i.e., the "anatomoclinical). The "focus of attention" continued to evolve in the nineteenth century with the incorporation of 'tissues' and 'cells' as the body's units for observation and experimentation.

The "focus of attention" is obtained by studying the morphology of the body's organs, tissues, and cells, the fundamental compartments in which the reactions of the body to injury are identified. The proper recognition of these manifestations of disease is achieved by observation with or without the assistance of technology and by nature and laboratory experimentation. Such recognition has demanded an evolution through centuries on the interpretation of findings by many savants that have left their names printed in the history of AP. The history of the recognition consists of overlapping interpretations about the nature of organs, tissues, and cells.

5.1 *Body Organs*

Aristotle (384-322 B.C.E.) and Galen classified the components of the human body into 'similar' and 'dissimilar' parts (King 1982, 172). The dissimilar parts were organs, limbs, and legs, and they called them Anhomoeomerous parts (Forrester 1994, 444-458). Particular attention to organs did not occur until the sixteenth century in Europe as the result of the introduction of post-mortem examinations in hospital patients. Autopsies brought notice to the fact that organic lesions could explain the cause of death and the manifestations of disease. In the following three centuries, such lesions became the answers to clinical questions, resulting in the creation of the anatomoclinical method. Pathological findings were analyzed in contrast to the normal, resulting in considering the organs 'the seat and cause of disease' (Morgagni [1769] 1983). But scientific curiosity had been going beyond the gross appearance of organs to their constituent parts.

5.2 *Fibers*

Interest on discovering the internal structure of the solid parts of the body goes back to the sixteenth century (Craigie 1851, 2-14). Jean Fernel and Gabriele Falloppia or Falloppio (1523-1562), in particular the latter, introduced the concept that the intimate invisible constitution of the human body was made of fibers. Before the sixteenth century, fibers in the human body were considered present only in tendons, muscles, and blood vessels (Robb-Smith 1970, 451). Falloppio considered that these fibers were visibly organized longitudinally into fibers, in two dimensions in textures, and in three dimensions into organs. The idea that they were made of atoms followed as an expression of the savants' opinion in the seventeenth and eighteenth centuries; that is, mechanism. To this conception it was added the idea of another context: 'vitalism', that gave functional properties to them (Lain Entralgo 1978, 272-273). Later, Haller considered the fibers made of molecules attached to each other by gluten. The corpuscular description that took the place of the fibrillar was the consequence of discoveries in physics (Canguilhem 2008, 33, 36). Additional authors replaced the molecules for globules. According to Virchow, this was an optical illusion produced when sun rays were the light source for the microscope (Virchow [1860] 1978, 25-26). Indeed, poor quality microscopes contributed to the erroneous interpretation of the observations. This is well described by Craigie, "… The solid parts are generally arranged in the form of collateral lines, sometimes oblique, sometimes perfectly parallel, sometimes mutually intersecting. Such lines are denominated fibres, and occasionally filaments" (Craigie 1851, 15). Chronologically, from 'fibers' the conception of the constitution of the human body was followed by that of textures (tissues). Nevertheless, the concept of fibers was only replaced by the 'cell' as the fundamental micro-structural component of the body in the nineteenth century.

5.3 *Tissues*

In Aristotle and Galen's times, the term Anhomoeomerous was contrasted with the thought that the whole human body is made of a series of components called homoeomerous parts, a conception that goes back to Anaxagoras (c. 500-c. 428 B.C.E.). Aristotle, and later Galen, listed the parts and assumed that they were constituted by the four elements (air, water, fire, and earth). Examples of homoeomerous parts were nerves, tendons, cornea, epidermis, etc. The thought eventually culminated during the eighteenth century with that of 'tissues' as a gross component of the internal structure of the human body (Forrester 1994, 444-458). The concept attempted to replace the 'organ' as the fundamental macro-structural component of the body.

As an evolving idea, the term 'tissue' must not be confused with its modern use that refers to a structure observed by light microscopy and that belongs to the science of histology. As a gross component of the body, in 1763, in the Netherlands, Andrew Bonn mentioned "tissues" and classified them into three textures: (1) mucous; (2) aponeurosis, periosteum, and perichondrium; and (3) serous and fibro-serous (Craigie 1851, 6-7, 2-14). In Britain, in 1788, J.C. Smythe (1741-1821) suggested the idea of 'tissue', and his name is always mentioned in relation to the history of textures. In 1790, he was the first to relate textures to inflammation in a paper published in *Medical Communications* of London (Craigie 1851, 7). In France, Ackerknecht calls attention to the work of Théophile de Bordeu (1722-1776) in "Recherches sur le tissu muqueux ou l'organe cellulaire" (Ackerknecht 1967, 52). Philippe Pinel (1745-1826) also dealt with the issue of tissues (Bichat [1827] 2009, 5).

Nevertheless, Bichat has received the entire credit for introducing the concept of 'tissue' in AP (Keel 2001, 255-279). His work is no more than a development of Bonn's work almost forty years later, though he only credits Haller and Pinel as precursors of the idea. Bichat, in *A Treatise on the Membranes* makes clear that he was informed about them, "it was in reading his work [Pinel's] that I first received this idea, in relation to membranes though many results appear here, as will be seen, very different from those he has announced" (Bichat [1813] 1987, 3-4, 22, 23). Others have written that Pinel called

Bichat's attention to the information in Morgagni's *Seats and Causes of Disease* that not all organs are involved in disease, but only certain parts of them (Martineau 1875, 331-332). Using only the tact, Bichat intended to create a new compartmentalization of the body different from the anatomic division by organs. He did that because he could have a better understanding of clinical manifestations and of disease's classifications through the participation of those membranes in the reaction to injury. Bichat introduced twenty-one different textures in organs, and this is the scheme around which the theme evolved. He introduced six in *Treatise on Membranes*, and expanded them to 21 in *General Anatomy*. (Bichat [1813] 1987; Bichat [1824] 2010, 39). By doing this, he revolutionized AP because he shifted the focus from organs to tissues. He went farther than previous authors by dividing textures into two categories. The first, he called 'general or generating system'. He did not name it, but reading the text indicates a second category that designate more or less the body's systems. This division is the first reference to the separation of AP into basic and clinical (Bichat [1824] 2010, 59; Laennec 1884, 46-47). Bichat further expanded in the separation in his other work, *Pathological Anatomy* (Bichat [1827] 2009). Bichat's conception of 'tissue' should not be confused with the modern understanding of tissue in histology. Although Bichat died in 1802, others followed his legacy.

Following Bichat's death, Laennec reinforced the importance of tissues on identifying the site of disease (Laennec 1884, 50-51). Other authors in France and Germany modified Bichat's classification but they were deficient because of being too simple or too complex (Craigie 1851, 2-14). On the other hand, there was no left definition of tissue. Bichat did not offer an exact meaning of the word. In the British literature, Craigie, in 1828, offered the following useful structural conception of tissue as understood at that time, "Most of the solids may be demonstrated to be penetrated by minute ramifying tubes or blood-vessels, ... The filamentous, fibrous, or globular or cellular arrangement (seen with the primitive microscopes), with the distribution of arborescent vessels, constitutes organization. The substances so constructed are named organized tissues (telæ, textus,) or textures, or simply tissues" (Craigie 1851, 15). Until the systematic introduction of better microscopes, this was the understanding of 'tissue' (Castiglioni 1941, 674). It was Virchow who moved the focus of attention to the 'cell' as the unit of organization in the human body's organs.

5.4 *The Cell*

Identification of a structural unit in biology is immersed in the men's natural curiosity to understand nature. A true inquiry on this issue began with the invention of lenses that augmented the observer's magnification beyond the naked eye. It was Antonie Philips van Leeuwenhoek (1632-1723), a dutchman, who observed with his primitive microscope that the intimate structure of the body was made of globules. This occurred in the seventeenth century when he was corresponding with Robert Hooke (1635-1703) who was the curator of experiments at the Royal Society (Croft 2006, 11; Snyder

2015, 10). Hooke is credited for being the first to use the term "cell", introducing it in 1665 to refer to spaces seen in cork and vegetables under the microscope. The spaces were also described by Malpighi in 1675 and Nehemiah Grew (1641-1712) in 1682. A review of Hooke's book, *Micrography*, revealed that in observation XVIII, he not only described and named the spaces but also gave them functional importance in relation to the circulation of sap in plants. He then compared this circulation to that of arteries and veins in animals (Hooke 1667, 112-121). When observing the spaces, Hooke did not think of them as the basic structures of the animal body because that idea was not prevalent at the time. It had to wait until the early nineteenth century when microscopic observations connected those spaces to the basic structural units of the body. The connection was possible by then because there was consensus on the existence of a basic body's structure (Harris 2000, 1-3).

Botanists were also researching the same theme, and by the end of the eighteenth century had a clear idea that their unit of structure was also the cell, but as understood today. Botany was a well-developed science, but there was no communication between botanists, zoologists, and physicians, in spite of the fact that many zoologists were also physicians (Harris 2000, 51, 53). These developments prevailed for some years until 1839, when German students of Johannes Müller brought a new attention to the theme.

The great contribution of Müller's students - Theodor Schwann, Robert Remak, and Rudolph Virchow - can be summarized as follows. The interpretation of the nature of the spaces described by Hooke began to change when

Robert Brown (1773-1858) discovered the nucleus in 1831 and Gabriel Valentin discovered the nucleolus in 1836 (Oertel 1927, 14). Simultaneously, Jacob Schleiden (1804-1881), a botanist, described the formation of new cells from the nucleus that he called cytoblast in 1838. After conversing with Schleiden, Theodor Schwann (1810-1882) proposed a similar mechanism of formation of new cells a year later. This mechanism considered such origin from nuclei present in an amorphous extravascular mass that he called cytoblastema; that is, it was a form of spontaneous generation (Garrison 1929, 454-455). In 1841 and 1852, Robert Remak (1815-1865) questioned this view and, using his studies on red blood cells, he proposed that cells arise from other cells by binary fission; a process already accepted by botanists. Then, Virchow took Remak's contribution, popularized it in pathology, and gained the credit for it. This was the beginnings of cellular pathology at the middle of the nineteenth century (Rather 1978, 84-87; Harris 2000).

By the last quarter of the nineteenth century, the cell was accepted as the unit of the body's structure in Britain as described in Green's textbook published in 1881 (Green 1881). One can also assume the same acceptance in North America given the book's popularity. Green wrote, "... the cell is the seat of nutrition and function; and further, that each individual cell is itself an independent organism, endowed with those properties, and capable of exhibiting those active changes which are characteristic of life. Every organized part of the body is either cellular or is derived from cells, and the cells themselves originate from pre-existing cells, and under no circumstances do they originate de novo. Whilst therefore the whole body is made up of cells, or of substances derived from cells, and the cell is itself the ultimate morphological element which is capable of exhibiting manifestations of life, ..." (20). The concept continued evolving and, once established, the cell was recognized as the unit of study in pathology (i.e., cellular pathology) in spite of the fact that by 1927, there still existed the belief that cell divided indirectly (by mitosis) and directly (by amitosis). Amitosis was considered the method of division in fully differentiated somatic cells (Oertel 1927, 217-218).

5.5 *Conclusions*

The morphological bases of AP were set by the second half of the nineteenth century when organs, tissues, and cells were properly identified and recognized as the site of disease. Organs came to attention after the 1500s as a result of the performance of autopsies. The organs, as a component of the solid parts of the body, were assumed to be made of fibers, fibrils, and corpuscles (atoms, molecules, and globules). To this assumption followed the idea of tissue as a component of the internal structure of the body, a concept popularized by Bichat in the first half of the nineteenth century. Bichat's terminology, however, did not refer to the modern application of the term in histology. Then, in the second half of the same century, Virchow introduced the cell as the fundamental unit of the body's structure. These developments, attributed to particular individuals, in reality were supported by the contributions of numerous savants. Organ/tissue/cell constitute a 'focus of attention' that coincided with the development of a method, both fulfilling the minimum requirements to consider the field of knowledge, in this case AP, a science.

CHAPTER 6

THE ANATOMOCLINICAL METHOD

The origin of modern AP can be described as an accumulation of specialized knowledge resulting from the evolution of scientific medical thought from the 1500s to the 1700s. During this period, morphological findings at autopsy, the 'focus of attention', began to be correlated with signs and symptoms, evolving into a new methodology to evaluate disease, the 'anatomoclinical method'. It offered answers to clinical questions different from those provided with Galen's humouralism. This accomplishment was achieved in 1761 by G. B. Morgagni's seminal publication, *Seats and Causes of Disease* in which he recapitulated the method since its beginnings in the 1500s.

The anatomoclinical method is a strategy that explains disease and corresponds to the positive phase of positivism. Humouralism represented the previous phase, the metaphysical. The successful replacement by the anatomoclinical method of humouralism was a progressive event that took two and a half centuries. Although there were attempts to replace it with other models lacking an anatomical basis, they were unsuccessful.

Eventually the correlation of anatomical findings with signs and symptoms overcame any other approach. The extraordinary importance of this history resides on the fact that the combination of the anatomoclinical method with a focus of interest, both resulting from the systematic practice of autopsies on medical practice, gave origin to the science of AP.

6.1 *Galen's Humouralism*

Galen's influence on medicine extended from the second century C.E. until the eighteenth, albeit with less force since the sixteenth century. His influence can be summarized in two areas, anatomy/physiology and humouralism. His anatomy started to be modified, and eventually abolished, by the contributions of Andreas Vesalius's *De humani corporis fabrica libri septem* published in 1543; his physiology was challenged by William Harvey's *Exercitatio anatomica de motu cordis et sanguinis* (Movement of the Heart and Blood in Animals), known as *De motu cordi*, in 1628 (Harvey [1628] 1963). In the following couple of centuries, physicians expanded on Vesalius and Harvey's contributions, increasing the knowledge that eventually made Galen's influence on anatomy/physiology disappear.

Galen's humouralism, on the other hand, proposed that four body's humors (red blood, yellow and black bile, and phlegm) and four human temperaments (sanguine, choleric, melancholic and phlegmatic) were kept in equilibrium by heat generated in the left ventricle of the heart from the action of the pneuma (air) and foods brought from the environment. When the system was in equilibrium, the result was health; alterations in the system resulted in disease (Rothschuh 1973, 5). Galen's explanations focused attention on the body fluids and were neither anatomic nor based on experimentation. However, they were viewed as satisfactory. Humouralism was unchallenged until the 16th century.

6.2 *Initial Attempts to Replace Humouralism*

Galen's humouralism began to have its detractors and challengers in the sixteenth century. The most famous was Theophrastus Bombastus von Hohenheim (1493-1541), also known as Paracelsus. He proposed a model based on the observation of nature that was a mixture of religion, magic, natural philosophy, and medicine. He opposed the idea that an imbalance of humors produced disease by postulating that specific diseases made the body feel ill. Consequently, treatments were designed to find specific drugs to treat specific conditions. Paracelsus' work undermined the existent theory of medicine but not its practice (Sudhoff 1926, 275-285; King 1971, 88-95; Hannam 2011, 247-250, 265).

A series of authors after Paracelsus made important contributions to the investigation of the nature of disease; that is, its essential qualities. Although, in some publications, their contributions were considered "systems of medicine," they were not. Their contributions, mainly through the introduction of experimentation, advanced the understanding of the function of the human body in health and disease. To name a few, one could mention

Harvey, René Descartes (1596-1650), Jan Baptist van Helmont (1580-1644), Thomas Willis (1621-1675), and Thomas Sydenham (1624-1689). To them, it followed the 'systematists'.

The so-called 'systematists' of the eighteenth century proposed "theoretical (rationalist) medical systems" whereby non-anatomic speculation based on misunderstood scientific facts gave origin to functional explanations of health and disease (Porter 1997, 246-252, 260, 262). The systems were widely used and the result of naturalistic explanations of phenomena promoted by the Enlightenment, the scientific advances brought about by the Scientific Revolution, and the influence of rationalistic thinking (Chambers et al. 1983, 633). The contributions of Stahl, Hoffman, Cullen, and Brown are illustrations of these systems.

Georg Ernst Stahl (1660-1734) created a system that considered the existence of an "anima," a principle identified as nature. This principle acted through the circulatory system to create movements in organs that maintained life (health). Since the natural tendency of the body was towards decomposition and putrefaction, the anima protected against this natural tendency. Disease arose from blood stasis in the vessels, with the anima making every possible effort to restore normal movements and, consequently, bringing back health (life). Stahl did not believe in anatomy, but his importance rested on the influence that his ideas had on what was later called 'vitalism' by Joseph Barthez (1734-1806) (Castiglioni 1941, 583-584). In contrast to Stahl, Friedrich Hoffman (1660-1742) created a system based on mechanical foundations. Life was movement and could be measured. He based his proposal on the conception that the body was made of fibres that could dilate and contract as a result of the action of an ether-like fluid, a vital principle present in the nervous system. He called that property, tonus. Any alteration of the tonus caused disease; contraction produced acute diseases whereas dilation produced chronic diseases (Garrison 1929, 314; Singer and Underwood 1962, 148; King 1971, 125-136). William Cullen (1712-1790) expanded on the idea that the action of the nervous system maintains the tonus of the body's solid parts according to the kind of external stimuli (Castiglioni 1941, 585). John Brown (1735-1788), a disciple of Cullen, moved his attention to the excitability of tissues in response to external stimulation. Diseases could be either "sthenic" or "asthenic" depending on the tissues' responses to increased or decreased stimulation, and were, therefore, treated accordingly (Garrison 1929, 314-315).

6.3 *A Method to Answer Clinical Questions*

In parallel to the developments from the sixteenth to the eighteenth centuries, a methodology to answer clinical questions resulted from the practice of autopsies in academic medicine and eventually replaced humouralism. The method was problem-oriented and consisted of three steps: obtaining the patient's history and her/his main clinical problems; performing an autopsy with its purpose to investigate findings related to the clinical problems; and correlating anatomical findings to signs and symptoms as cause-effect in order to explain etiopathogenesis. It has been since known as the 'anatomoclinical method'.

The gradual development of the method is traced in three books published from the sixteenth to the middle third of the eighteenth century (Long [1928] 1965). They were: *De Abditis Nonnullis Ac Mirandis Morborum et Sanationum Causis* (On Some Hidden and Remarkable Causes of Disease and Recovery) by Antonio Benivieni, published in the sixteenth century (1507) by his brother; *Sepulchretum sive Anatomia Practica* (Sepulchretum) by Theophilus Bonetus, published in the seventeenth century (1679); and *De Sedibus et Causis Morborum per Anatomen Indagitis* (The Seats and Causes of Disease Investigated by Anatomy) by G. B. Morgagni, published in the eighteenth century (1761). These three books are representative of similar publications at the time.

Several other books dealing with specific organs were concurrently being published. Examples are works by Marco Aurelio Severino (1580-1656), Giovanni Maria Lancisi (1654-1720), and Antonio Maria Valsalva (1666-1723). They not only reported morbid changes that could be considered part of AP today but also had their correlations with symptoms. The difference is that Benivieni, Bonet, and Morgagni included cases from the whole body rather than from specific organs (Singer & Underwood 1962, 628-629).

Beniviene's *Hidden and Causes of Disease* already contained the approach that eventually would evolve into the new methodology. It is a collection of 111 cases, each case beginning with a short clinical history; brief autopsy findings were described for thirteen unusual cases. Clinical aspects received more attention because the intention was clinical, not pathological. Benivieni focused on explaining the cause of death to satisfy a clinical curiosity. The book was published thirty-six years before Vesalius' *Fabrica* (1543) and, therefore, the interpretations were based on medieval anatomical criteria and humouralism (Vesalius 1944). Yet, the beginning of the anatomoclinical method was suggested with the inclusion of clinical history, post-mortem findings, and their correlation. Benivieni was not alone with his publication. In 1554, Jean Fernel (1506-1558), who introduced the term "pathology" in its modern sense, wrote *Pathologia* (Sherrington 1946, 101, 184-185). In the text, the description of the method was more developed than Benivieni's.

Bonetus' *Sepulchretum* followed Benivieni's in the next (seventeenth) century. It consisted of four books containing a collection of already published cases from the sixteenth and seventeenth centuries. It was organized by signs and symptoms and incorporated more extensive comments on autopsy findings than Benivieni's (Nicholls 1927, 463-466; Irons 1942, 623-665). Although it had a clinical rather than a pathological approach, the *Sepulchretum* contained the genesis of the method in a more advanced form than Fernel's *Pathologia*. However, the treatise included many factual errors, and explanations were still based on humouralism (Cunningham 2010, 193-194).

In the eighteenth century, Albrecht von Haller (1708-1777) produced a collection of post-mortem examinations in 1756 that he titled *Pathological Observations* (Haller 1756). Samuel Clossy (1724-1786) did the same in 1763 with his text, *Observations on Some of the Diseases of the Parts of the Human Body*. In 1767, following the style of the *Sepulchretum*, Joseph Lieutaud (1703-1789) published *An Anatomico-medical History* (Cunningham 2010, 196). However, in 1761, it was Morgagni who made a full and systematic description of the method in his monumental work *De Sedibus et Causis Morborum per Anatomen Indagatis* (Seats and Causes of Disease).

Morgagni's book is more like to a clinical medicine text with extensive pathological descriptions than a pathology book. Morgagni collected all the information he could about the practice of medicine by the middle of the eighteenth century. The text incorporates etiology, epidemiology, pathogenesis, clinical symptoms and signs, autopsy findings, prognoses and treatments of disease as known at that time. Knowledge is organized by clinical cases and follows the structure of modern clinical medical textbooks. Morgagni also classified his cases by 'cause', an important advance because causality is mandatory to consider a field of knowledge scientific. All pathological descriptions intend to explain the clinical case (Morgagni [1769] 1983). By doing this, he introduced an updated version of the anatomoclinical method with its three components: clinical description, autopsy findings, and anatomoclinical correlation. Morgagni is considered the founder of AP in the medical literature.

6.4 Conclusions

Creation of the anatomoclinical method was indispensable for the dawn of the new discipline of AP.

The method did not develop from nowhere. Evolution of physicians' mentality played an unquestionable role as unraveled in the successive publications of Benivieni, Bonetus, and Morgagni. Only then could the explanation of signs and symptoms according to Galen's humouralism be replaced by their interpretation according to organ's morphology. Disease was then understood on the bases of observation/analogy and no longer on speculations.

From these considerations, one can conclude that the origin of AP spanned from the 1500s to the 1700s, and it occurred when there existed a "focus of attention" (body organs) and a methodology (the anatomoclinical method). Both conditions were necessary to establish a new field of study as a science, a science that eventually replaced Galen's humouralism. The occurrence was supported by a parallel evolution of medical thinking.

CHAPTER 7

THE FIRST ATLASES OF ANATOMIC PATHOLOGY

Book production flourished after Johannes Gutenberg (ca. 1398-1468) (re) introduced the movable type press, which was four centuries after the Chinese had invented it along with paper (Trombley 2011, 89). The new inventions facilitated diffusion of knowledge using print medium. However, there were limitations on printing drawings, so European museums became the institutions that collected specimens for examination. In the sixteenth and seventeenth century, private collections of 'natural history', an old term for 'science', appeared with the main objective of collecting rare and interesting specimens. Museums competed with books (McNeely 2008, 142, 145). In the eighteenth century in England, there were several private museums, the William and John Hunter's museums being the ones that had the most complete collections of pathological human and animal material (Moore 2005). By the dawn of the nineteenth century, engraving was available and museums would become the source of specimens for elaborating atlases.

Atlases appeared in Britain in 1803. The first was Matthew Baillie's *A Series of Engravings*, followed by Robert Carswell's *Pathological Anatomy* in 1838, known also as the *Fasciculus* (Hollman 1995, 566-570; Karamanou et al. 2012, 400-402; Bertolini 2015, 209-242; Spear 2018, 622-631). Between Baillie's and Carswell's publications there were two other atlases published in Great Britain. One appeared in 1830 and was titled *A Vade-Mecum of Morbid Anatomy, Medical and Chirurgical with Pathological Observations and Symptoms*. Its author was anonymous and, according to the *Lancet*, it was of lower quality than Baillie's *A Series of Engravings* (Cunningham 2010, 2, 32). In 1834, the Dublin physician James Hope (1801-1841) published another atlas on systemic (clinical) pathology. It had 260 pages and 48 plates. Each plate showed several figures, the majority in colour but also some in black & white (Hope 1834).

The contribution of atlases is relevant because they overcame the limitation of only having museums to study gross specimens. Baillie's and Carswell's atlases illustrating gross morphology fulfilled the need of anatomists and anatomic pathologists. Their subject matter, the technology involved in their elaboration, and their comparisons allow us to infer their relevance upon the origin of anatomic pathology in the English literature.

7.1 *Who Was Matthew Baillie*

Matthew Baillie (1761-1823) was born in Scotland and died in London. His life is well described in the literature (Garrison 1929, 354-355; Rodin 1973, 5-18;

Porter 1997, 264). He was the son of Reverend James Baillie and Dorothy Hunter-Baillie, the sister of the Hunter brothers. At the age of 18 and after the death of his father in 1779 his mother sent him to live with William Hunter, beginning an association that would mark his future professional life. William, in turn, sent Matthew to Oxford. After his return in 1780, he was incorporated into the staff of William's Windmill Street School as an assistant. Concurrently, Matthew was a pupil of his uncle John at St. George's Hospital. In the Board of Governors' Minutes of the Hospital in 1788, Baillie appears listed as a physician, not a surgeon (Lawrence 1996, 53). After William's death in 1783, Baillie became the heir of the school, and him and William Cruikshank directed the school for the next sixteen years. During that period, Matthew received degrees from Oxford, was inducted as a Fellow into the College of Physicians of London in 1789, and practiced medicine at St. George's Hospital.

Baillie initially published *Morbid Anatomy of Some of the Most Important Parts of the Human Body* (Baillie [1812] n.d.) in 1793, the year of John Hunter's death. It is the first book published in modern AP (Long [1928] 1965, 93; Krumbhaar [1937] 1965, 170). Baillie, an Englishman, inverted Morgagni's analysis in his publication by focusing on the anatomical findings first and only secondarily on the clinical manifestations of disease. This approach called attention to the basic reactions of the body to injury; that is, basic science pathology. It was a success. The book was translated into German, French, Italian, and Russian, and inspired similar publications by Vogel, Meckel, Otto, and Cruveilhier in the next fifteen to twenty years

(Krumbhaar [1937] 1962). Baillie eventually abandoned his immediate interest in pathology and moved on to a very successful private practice. Contemporaries of Baillie attributed the success of his practice to the fame acquired from *Morbid Anatomy*. He was in private practice until his death in 1823 (Rodin 1973, 5-18).

7.2 *Baillie's Atlas: Organized by Organs*

Matthew Baillie published *A Series of Engravings* to complement the *Morbid Anatomy* ten years later. The atlas is also organized by organs, although he considered both works independent of each other (Baillie 1803, i, 5). The atlas is divided into ten fascicles, each one devoted to one or several organs. A fascicle consists of two parts: first, an introduction followed by a section named 'Plates'; and second, the engravings. The number of Plates in each fascicle ranges from six to nine, and each contains a short initial statement indicating its content. This is followed by a description as illustrated in Plate II of fascicle 1: "This Plate is intended to illustrate the diseased alterations of structure, to which the valves of the heart are subject. These consist chiefly in the valves becoming thick and opaque, or becoming ossified. ..." (13). Following these statements, there is a list of numbered figures that correspond to the figures in the engravings. Each figure contains an introductory short description of the specimen, for instance in Plate VI, "FIG. I. Represents the anterior view of the heart" (21). This is followed by a list of lettered legends that corresponds to explanations in the figures. The legends consist of short morphological statements frequently accompanied by an interpretation in which structural changes are emphasized, "E. The trunk of the pulmonary artery laid open, shewing a probe in it: it arises from the left ventricle" (21). Magnifying glasses are utilized to examine engravings (95). There are no reports of measurements; yet, occasionally there are references to chemical analyses (148, 149, 163). At the end of the last figure in a Plate, he mentions the source of the material and the bibliographic references when applicable; for example, "This heart has been already engraved, and an account of the case has been given by Dr. Samuel Foart Simmons, and of the dissection after death, by the late Mr. Watson, Surgeon of the Westminster Hospital. See *Medical Communications*, Vol I p. 228" (20). In general, explanations in each fascicle are simple and clear, based on 'common sense', and 'mechanical' in nature (87). Frequently, there is no clinical information, and only very occasionally are some physio-pathological considerations (23). The second part of each fascicle contains the engravings printed on separate pages in black and white. Each engraving shows more than one figure.

It has been said that Baillie obtained these illustrations from the Hunters' museums, a statement popular not only during his life but also in the literature that followed (Rodin 1973, 7-14). He was accused of basing his work on the specimens from William's collection. Baillie never denied these claims (Baillie [1812] n.d., x) and said that this was only partially true (Baillie [1803] n.d., 6). The accusations were not surprising given not only the expected envy of Baillie's success, but also their close association with his uncles. Out of the 187 specimens utilized, William Hunter's museum provided 101 (54%) and John Hunter had contributed 20 (11%), making an approximate contribution by both Hunters of 121, around two thirds of the total. The rest, a significant one third (66 or 35%), belonged to the author's personal collection, friends' collections, and other museums. He donated his collection of 1,281 morbid specimens to the Royal College of Physicians. The collection, later transferred to the Royal College of Surgeons, was destroyed in May 1941 during an air raid in World War II (Cunningham 2010, 2, 30). Carswell's specimens had a different source.

7.3 *Who Was Robert Carswell*

Robert Carswell (1793-1857), a clinician practicing pathology, was born in Scotland in 1793 – the year that Baillie published his *Morbid Anatomy* – and graduated M.D. in Glasgow in 1826. In his own words, he thanked Dr James Jeffray (1759-1848), Professor of Anatomy and Physiology at the University of Glasgow, "in directing my attention in a special manner to the study of Pathological Anatomy" (Carswell 1838, 8). Before and after graduation, he spent time in Paris elaborating drawings of morbid lesions, first commissioned by Dr John Thompson (1765-1846) and later on his own initiative. Carswell studied with Louis and Laennec and spent time at hospitals in Paris and Lyon. In 1828, he was appointed Chair of Pathology at University College in London at the same time that his teacher, John Thomson, was appointed at Edinburgh. These were the first Chairs of Pathology created in Great Britain. Carswell obtained the position because Johannes Meckel (1781-1833) did not accept the offer (Maulitz 1987, 146, 216-218). Yet, he did not take the possession until 1831 because he continued working on his drawings in Paris. In the *Fasciculus,* there are frequent references to Paris institutions, French authors, and French literature, indicating that the Paris School of medicine influenced him. In London, he devoted a decade working on the *Fasciculus* and the university's museum. After an unsuccessful medical practice and teaching, Carswell accepted an appointment as physician to the King of Belgium in 1840, dying there in 1857 (Payne n.d.; Maulitz 1987, 146, 222).

7.4 *Carswell's Atlas: Organized by Morbid Reactions*

Robert Carswell's *Pathological Anatomy,* known also as the *Fasciculus,* has two components, an extensive text and an atlas at the end in each of eleven fascicles (Carswell 1838; Hollman 1995; Karamanou et al. 2012, 400-402; Bertolini 2015; Spear 2018). The atlases are the focus of our attention. They consist of figures and generous descriptions, each one dedicated to one of the following morbid reactions: inflammation, analogous tissues, atrophy, hypertrophy, pus, mortification, haemorrhage, softening, melanoma, carcinoma, and tubercle. Each atlas is divided into four plates, with each plate containing several figures that illustrate the lesions, for a total of 269 figures in the whole book. The figures were obtained from engravings and are incredibly well presented in colour.

The figures are representative of the reactions and are outstanding. In addition to humans, they came from a variety of sources, such as rabbits, cows, horses, and monkeys, indicating that Carswell was practicing animal experimentation (Carswell 1838, 29, 85, 87, 215, 309, 310). Another source was the published literature (112, 113). The figures are described in detail and their interpretations are devoted to explaining morphological findings (27); for instance, "… In peritonitis, the inflammation generally commences, as has been stated, along the contiguous margins of the neighbouring folds of the intestine, and from thence proceeds over the surface in the direction in which the blood vessels are distributed. …" (28, 84, 264). Colour influences the interpretation of figures, "… there was effused blood, which preserved its red colour, the sudden death of the patient not having afforded time for the changes of colour which are observed to take place in this fluid under opposite circumstances, …" (217). Sometimes, colour changes are used to explain lesions (87). The microscope is not used, but measurements like lines and inches are included (237, 238).

The plentiful of descriptions serve as the explanation of the physiological manifestations of disease, as in the production of ascites due to obliteration by carcinomatous matter of the lumen of the vena porta without perforation, or obstruction by outside compression by the tumour (Carswell 1838, 265). Descriptions also clarify terminology. A term like 'pancreatic' refers to the appearance of a tumour, not to the body's organ (284). Otherwise, the term 'cell' is applied to anatomical spaces, such as the alveoli of the lung, spaces in the spleen, and spaces left by tissue's central necrosis (312).

Carswell's atlas offers hints, obtained through experience, that become advice on techniques to those performing autopsies. For instance, "Fig. 4 represents the chemical discolouration of the blood when effused beneath or on the surface of the peritoneum, and which by some pathologists has been confounded with true melanosis. ... from the action of the acid contents of the intestine ..." (Carswell 1838, 241). Although clinical information is very rarely given in the atlas, there are correlations of autopsy findings with ante-mortem surgical procedures (113). Another hint comes from the use of special techniques for investigation, such as injection of mercury in the mesentery's lacteals (311). These advances were made possible by the high quality of the figures in Carswell's and also Baillie's atlases, which were only achievable by the techniques of engraving.

7.5 *The Role of Technology in the Elaboration of the Atlases*

Atlases became necessary to maintain evidence given the conditions under which bodies to be autopsied were preserved. Because there was no refrigeration, examinations were performed in the winter months. Bodies were kept no more than five to eight days, and, during this time, physicians were actively participating in the post-mortems (Quinonez and McLendon 2011, 1591-1596). Consequently, illustrations of findings had great practical, legal, and didactic value. Nevertheless, atlases were not popular due to technical limitations. Baillie affirmed that engravings were found scattered in other kinds of publications; that they were expensive, difficult to acquire, and poor in details; and presented only the external surface and not the cross sections of the organs. According to him, none contained a similar collection of published engravings before his (Baillie [1803] n.d., 3-5).

The solution to these limitations had to be improvements on engraving; that is, the technique of carving a figure in a solid material with the purpose of printing it on paper later. This was achieved in Baillie's and Carswell's atlases. The technique, as described by Baillie, was performed in two steps: drawing and engraving proper (Baillie [1803] n.d., 6, 7). In the first step, the artist made a drawing of the specimen. In Baillie's atlas, William Clift (1755-1849) made the drawings. He had been John Hunter's assistant and curator of his museum (Singer and Underwood 1962, 171). In the second step, the same artist, or another artist, used a sharp instrument to carve the outline on a wood or metallic (usually copper) plate from which the printing on paper was obtained. Engravings in metal represented an improvement in the technique. Printing was in black-and-white or colour. Baillie explained his technical considerations for not using colour. He mentions that the colour of parts is lost in wet and dry preparations from which engravings are done and, therefore, the colour could only be represented from memory (Baillie [1803] n.d., 29).

Distinctly different from Baillie, Carswell coloured his plates. One can only imagine the technical difficulties of adding colour to the engraving plates. It was commonly made by hand painting the already elaborate plate with soluble vegetable dyes of different colours and intensities, where appropriate. Carswell did not give information of the process of engraving nor colouring. He only stated, "… to represent, by coloured delineations, the healthy and diseased appearances of the human body, …" (Carswell 1838, 8). The literature pictured Carswell as an excellent drawer; and from this, one can assume that he made the drawings. There is no information, though, if he also did the carving.

7.6 *Comparison between Baillie's and Carswell's Atlases*

Baillie's and Carswell's atlases show important distinctions. A fundamental one is an improvement on the quality of the illustrations by the use of colour in Carswell's, something not seen in Baillie's black-and-white pictures. However, the detail is better in Baillie's illustrations. Colour is not the only dissimilarity. The organization of *A Series of Engravings* and the *Fasciculus* is different. The first is arranged by 'body organs' whereas the second is by 'morbid reactions' and, therefore, akin to basic science pathology. Baillie's atlas was written independent of the text of *Morbid Anatomy*, whereas Carswell incorporated the text and the atlas into the *Fasciculus*, making the information complementary (Carswell 1838, 28). Differences are also noted in descriptions and editing. Carswell's descriptions are more elaborate, attentive to detail, and contain technical hints for those practicing autopsies (287). It includes seventy-two figures more than Baillie's does; that is, it is more extensively illustrated. *A Series of Engravings*, on the other hand, was better edited; although occasional errors in numbering of black-and-white figures are noted, something not found in the *Fasciculus* (168). In Carswell's, there are occasionally figures poorly distributed in one plate. In spite of these observations, both atlases represent the accepted level of knowledge at that time.

7.7 Conclusions

The evaluation and comparison of the content of the first two valuable pathology atlases published in the English literature indicate that their illustrations competed with the visual inspection of the museum's specimens. Given that museums were located in particular geographical locations and may have had limited access, the diffusion of the written word in the form of atlases overcame that limitation. In addition, the lack of refrigeration for preserving bodies for post-mortem examination added another disadvantage that could be overcome through these kinds of publications. The comparison of both atlases reveals that Baillie's *A Series of Engravings* is the first printed visual study of the organic lesions produced by disease. On the other hand, the atlas section of Carswell's *Fasciculus* is a systematic morphological evaluation of the reactions of the body to injury as known at that time and the true first document of basic science pathology in the English literature. Besides their content, both publications offer the opportunity to appraise the application of engraving, one of the first techniques ancillary used in AP before the systematic introduction of light microscopy. Eventually, engraving became standard in all publications in this field. Based on these considerations, one may conclude that the two atlases were relevant not only for the diffusion of pathologic knowledge but also in popularizing the new science of AP in the English-speaking world.

CHAPTER 8

VIRCHOW'S "CELLULAR PATHOLOGY"

Morgagni, an Italian, published in 1761 *The Seats and Causes of Disease Investigated by Anatomy* (Morgagni [1769] 1983), a book that transcended pathology due to its relevance in the history of modern medicine. There is general acceptance that this is the first treatise in which one can find the origin of pathology. Undoubtedly, the book set the 'focus of attention' and the 'anatomoclinical method' with its three components: clinical description, autopsy findings, and their correlation. Morgagni paid attention to clinical (systemic) pathology, focusing his analyses on signs and symptoms first and anatomical findings second. Others consider that Baillie's (1761-1823) *Morbid Anatomy of Some of the Most Important Parts of the Human Body* (Baillie [1812] n.d.) is the first book published in AP (Long [1928] 1965, 93; Krumbhaar [1937] 1965, 170). Baillie, a Scotsman, inverted Morgagni's analysis in his 1793 publication by focusing on the anatomical findings first. This called attention to the basic reactions of the body to injury; that is, basic science pathology. The issue was later developed by Bichat,

Laennec, and others in Paris. Finally, in 1858, Virchow, a German, published his *Cellular Pathology as Based upon Physiological and Pathological Histology* (Virchow [1860] 1978). In his lectures, he introduced 'cellular pathology' and contributed to establish the experimental basis for studying the reactions of the body to injury that he called 'Pathological Processes'.

The origin of any science is always a complex phenomenon. In the case of AP, savants from other European countries were concomitantly contributing to the knowledge of the nascent science in the first half of the nineteenth century. One cannot ignore the treatises of Gabriel Andral (1797-1876) and Jean Cruveilhier (1791-1874) in France; Johann Friedrich Georg Christian Martin Lobstein (1777-1835) and Johann Friedrich Meckel, the Younger (1781-1833) in Germany; and Carl von Rokitansky (1804-1878) in Vienna.

Cellular Pathology consists of a series of twenty lectures directed to practicing physicians. In them, the author proposes a 'theory of life', the cellular nature of all vital processes, upon which pathology, in his opinion, should be based (Virchow [1860] 1978, vii). This is the issue that has received the most attention in subsequent years. However, at the end of his last lecture, Virchow also refers to 'Principles' he defends that he demonstrated in his presentations. A careful analysis of the text also reveals his contributions in experimentation, anatomoclinical correlation, and microscopy. His book, therefore, can be considered a culmination in the progressive evolution of knowledge that finally set the foundation of modern AP. Being Virchow the one who introduced the systematic study of the foundational knowledge, (i.e., the Pathological Processes), I will focus on *Cellular Pathology* and in Virchow's legacy.

8.1 *Who Was Rudolph Virchow*

Rudolf Ludwig Karl Virchow (1821-1902) was born in Prussia. In 1843, he graduated medical school in Berlin where he began his career as Prosector at the Charité Hospital. In 1847, he co-founded the journal *Virchow's Archiv*, one of his important contributions to AP and medicine. In 1848, the Prussian government commissioned him to investigate an epidemic of typhus in Upper Silesia. His report was critical of the government and, as a result, he was obliged to abandon his position at the Charité the year after. Through the influence of the obstetrician Scanzoni, he was appointed chair of AP at Würzburg, Bavaria, where he gained prestige due to his knowledge and abilities as a teacher. Seven years later, he was recruited back to Berlin and appointed Professor of Pathology at the University and Director of the Pathological Institute at the Charité, a position specially created for him. At the time of the publication of *Cellular Pathology* in 1858, Virchow was Public Professor in Ordinary of Pathological Anatomy, General Pathology, and Therapeutics in the University of Berlin; Director of the Pathological Institute; and Physician to the Charité. After the publication, fame followed him (Garrison 1929, 569-572; Castiglioni 1941, 695-698; Putschar 1973, i-viii).

As a pathologist, Virchow's contributions were based on observation as a method. He used gross, micro, and a few rudimentary experimental techniques for today's standards (e.g., direct application of chemicals [acetic acid] to tissues). He had a particular ability for attention to details and a capacity for synthesis, characteristics that he later applied to archeology. His cellular theory's arguments were supported by experimental procedures, analogy, and use of morphology to explain cause-effect relationships (Garrison 1929, 569-572; Castiglioni 1941, 695-698; Putschar 1973, i-viii).

Virchow exceled not only in pathology but also in politics, anthropology, and medical history. In politics, he was a reformer elected parliamentarian in the Prussian Lower House and had an active role rivaling Otto von Bismark (1815-1898). Anthropology was his hobby and, of his 2000 publications, half were dedicated to physical and cultural anthropology. In medical history, he wrote articles on the hospitals of the Middle Ages and biographies of Johannes Müller, Morgagni, and Schönlein. Virchow also gained notoriety by discrediting the remnants of the blastema theory, at this time propounded by the Vienna School of medicine, and by disproving Cruveilher's phlebitis theory (Garrison 1929, 569-572; Castiglioni 1941, 695-698; Putschar 1973, i-viii).

8.2 *The Lectures*

Cellular Pathology consists of twenty lectures delivered by Virchow to practicing physicians at the Pathological Institute of Berlin during the months of February, March, and April of 1858 (Virchow [1860] 1978). In them, he proposes a 'theory of life' - the cellular nature of all vital processes - upon which pathology should be based. From the theory must follow the interpretation of the mechanisms and chemistry of the cell, both physiological and pathological. The emphasis contrasted with the existent neo-humouralistic explanations of life. The lectures were the ultimate successful effort to eliminate vitalism as a doctrine of life (Bignold et al. 2008, 140-146).

Being a hallmark in the history of AP, Virchow's lectures represent the beginnings of cellular pathology. In the twenty lectures, he uses a systematic approach to identify the cell as the body's centre of activity. In the presentations, the basis of each theme is previous knowledge (history, theories). By criticizing previous knowledge when pertinent, the cellular theory was introduced. The arguments to support the theory were based on current experimental procedures. In short, the driving attention was 'cells', 'function', and 'morphology'. Virchow did not take credit for the whole content of the lectures. In the preface of the second edition in 1859, he modestly states, "… those who had kept up their knowledge by reading the current medical literature would here find but little that was new to them" (Virchow [1860] 1978, xi). He was well informed not only of the German literature but also of other European countries. It is in these lectures that he put forward the term "Pathological Processes/Reactions."

Cellular Pathology displays one hundred forty-four microscopic preparations using engraving in wood, a presentation supportive of the historical attribution to Virchow of being the one who introduced the systematic application of light microscopy in pathology. The highest microscopic magnifying power was 300X, and the observations were associated with gross manifestations.

Lecture I is an introduction to the cell theory. Virchow credits Schwann and Schleiden for introducing it but discredits Schwann's proposal that cells arise from a cytoblastema. It is in this Lecture that he lays down the bases of pathology based on the cell theory. Since Virchow did not consider the content of the lectures totally original, he acknowledges that he was summarizing the knowledge of the last fifteen years to which he added his own experimental experiences, his vision of the cell as the site of the lesions in pathology, and the recognition of the value of histology and the systematic use of the microscope on AP.

Lectures II and III deal with physiological and pathological tissues. In Lecture II, Virchow discusses the previous beliefs on the intimate nature of the body, that is, fibres and globules. According to him, these beliefs were interfering with the histological classification of tissues and with the explanation of the Pathological Processes. He also states "that no development of any kind begins de novo, and consequently as to reject the theory of equivocal [spontaneous] generation." And very importantly, "When a cell arises, there a cell must have previously existed (omnis cellula e cellula), just as an animal can spring only from an animal, a plant only from a plant…. an eternal law of continuous development prevails" (Virchow [1860] 1978, 27-28). In contrast to Bichat who identified twenty-one tissues based on texture, in Lecture II he classifies tissues by histology instead and uses the cell and its relationship with neighboring cells as the basis for the classification.

In Lecture III, Virchow introduces, without defining, several Pathologic Processes, such as degeneration, atrophy, hypertrophy, neoplasm, tubercle; but, different from tradition, all of them are interpreted from the point of view of the 'cell'. It is in this Lecture that Virchow honors the title of the book by relating structure with function when referring for the first time to a particular pathological entity, i.e., 'progressive (fatty) atrophy'. He does not define it but explains its morphology in skeletal muscle that consists of a linear arrangement of fat globules in between the intracellular fibrils of the muscle. By diminishing the number of fibrils, the muscle diminishes in size (i.e., atrophy) and its contractile capacity also decreases. He also redefines several terms like hypertrophy, hyperplasia, and fatty degeneration as processes occurring at the cellular level. In this Lecture, Virchow also separates 'pathological tissues' from 'pathological structures' (variations of the normal). Virchow's understanding of 'pathological tissues' is, "… those only can be meant which really constitute pathological new formations, and not physiological parts which have simply undergone alteration in consequence of some deviation from the normal processes of nutrition" (Virchow [1860] 1978, 60).

Lectures IV, V and VI address nutrition. In Lecture IV, Virchow reinforces the importance of nutrition to the anatomical relation between blood vessels and cells and, from his experimental results, continues illustrating the replacement of old concepts using the cell theory and the microscope. In Lecture V, Virchow re-interprets histology using experimental techniques and the existence of cells. As an illustration of the re-interpretation, he describes the dartos of the scrotum. He makes functional conclusions about this muscle using a histological description, the application of carmine and acetic acid to stain it and distinguish it from connective tissue, and the demonstration of their nuclei. He also speculates about the limitations of the observations offered by the microscope at the obtained magnifications. In Lecture VI, Virchow introduces a model of injury in which nutrition plays a pivotal role. The basic mechanism of damage is nutrition (or lack of), and it is here that blood vessels and capillaries play a crucial role. This mechanism is stimulated by injury that alter the nutrition of tissues and eventually damage the cells.

It is in Lecture VI that Virchow criticizes Rokitansky's theory of dyscrasias. Rokitansky presented a variation of spontaneous generation and humouralism called neo-humouralism. He considered that an initial alteration of the proteins in the blood produced something similar to fibrin. This substance filtered into the extra-vascular space and formed a blastema. It was in this formation that abnormal cells originated, giving rise to disease. Using extensive experimentation and those of other authors like C. Bernard on the sugar metabolism in the liver, Virchow states, "My cellulo-pathological views differ from the humoro-pathological ones essentially in this, that I do not regard the blood as a permanent tissue, in itself independent, regenerating and propagating itself out of itself, but as in a state of constant dependence upon other parts. ... The essential point, therefore, is to search for the local origins of the different dyscrasiae, ..." (Virchow [1860] 1978, 130-131).

Lectures VII to XI study the blood, the lymphatic system, and their pathology. Lecture VII is a systematic and detailed study of the blood and its components; that is, plasma, red blood cells, and white (colourless) blood cells, with emphasis on the use of the microscope. The text of these lectures looks like a book on blood physiology.

In Lecture VIII, Virchow extends his studies on the blood to the lymphoid system. The first part of the Lecture is devoted to fibrine. He postulates the existence of a precursor of fibrin that he names 'fibrinogenous substance' that transforms into fibrin under the action of air. This substance may be present in blood or brought to it by the lymph. Then Virchow moves on to leucocytosis and leukemia and their relation to lymph and lymphatic glands, claiming that he had introduced both terms. His definition of leucocytosis contains two aspects: the increase in the number of cells in blood and the compromise of the lymphatic glands. In addition to experimentation, he also emphasizes his experiences with autopsies and, in support of the cell theory, insinuates that the properties of red blood cells, through division, are transmitted from one cell to another.

Lecture IX is about pyemia and the origin of the white blood cells in the spleen, the intestinal follicles, the tonsils, the follicles of the root of the tongue, and the thymus gland. Virchow also describes the physiopathology of the lymphatic system and uses metastatic breast cancer in the axilla and the syphilitic bubo to support his position that lymph nodes offer protection. His personal experience consisted of observations made in pathological material. In this Lecture, he describes errors in interpretation by others; specifically, of assuming that the increased number of pus-corpuscles in blood is due to reabsorption of pus and not production of cells by lymph nodes, the argument that he supports.

In Lecture X and around the topic of pyemia, Virchow introduces the concept of thrombosis, embolism, and metastatic deposits, indicating the importance of the microscope in the interpretation of biological phenomena, in this case, of a thrombus. He revisits the issue of dyscrasias that he considers a local phenomenon not transported by blood, except in the case of metastases and pyemia. When explaining tumor deposition away from the primary and escaping intermediate organs (lungs, for example), he postulates that a fluid is transported distantly from the primary and excites malignant changes there. He links cancer metastasis with pyaemia physio-pathologically and accepts that the unit of cancer is a cell, but he attributes the reason of a metastatic deposit to the cell's environment. The Lecture emphasizes two forms of investigation: microscopical and chemical.

In the first part of Lecture XI, Virchow discusses melanin and other ill-defined pigments present in the blood's cells, followed by the origin of these cells and their role in pathology. At every possible occasion he correlates findings with clinical symptoms and makes physiological conclusions from clinical (and autopsy) experiences. The bases of his inferences, therefore, are anatomoclinical observations. He is careful with his conclusions when they are not supported by facts, and puts emphasis on the role of the microscope. In the second part of this Lecture, Virchow focuses on the peripheral nervous system. He applied chemicals to tissues, and then examined them with the microscope as a way to advance histopathology. It is in this Lecture that Virchow introduces the term "myeline" to refer to a substance he obtained by chemical extraction from several tissues and considered to be lecithine. He called the disappearance of myeline in the peripheral nerves 'grey atrophy' or 'gelatinous degeneration'.

Lectures XII and XIII are about the nervous system. Lecture XII is a continuation of the previous Lecture. Addressing the peripheral nervous system, Virchow comments on the limitation of the experimental methodology and how such limitation limits the interpretation of function. He points this out because, at every opportunity, he tried to correlate structure with function using other investigators' discoveries to support his interpretation if necessary.

In Lecture XIII, Virchow continues his presentation on the nervous system with the study of the spinal cord and brain. The majority of the Lecture is about the anatomo-histology of the nervous system, both peripheral and central, and only occasionally are pathological changes mentioned. Virchow links gross observation with the innovation introduced by the light microscopic examination, focusing on the cell. This examination is supplemented with chemical tests using iodine and sulphuric acid, and comparative anatomy. He unifies the concept of connective tissue in all sites of the body, including its role in cancer and its presence in the central nervous system as "neuron-glia," another term introduced by him.

Lecture XIV deals with 'irritability' and the issue of 'life'. According to Virchow, there are three kinds of irritation: functional, nutritive, and formative. As examples of the action of irritability, he mentions hypertrophy, inflammation, and cloudy swelling. He demonstrates experimentally that neuropathologists have been wrong because inflammation resulting from irritation is not the result of nerve action. Virchow supports these statements with the experimental evidence by Traube in France, by Bernard in Utrecht, and by himself. He uses this evidence to attack the neuro-pathologists' argument that "irritation produces inflammation through the medium of the nerves" instead of its action on cells. To support the latter, he adds that irritation in the skin and the cornea affect the part directly irritated and not the area supplied by a particular nerve. Therefore, he concludes that the 'cells' are the last level of biological organization on which the effects of irritation occur. Virchow also addresses the issue of life. Contrary to common beliefs that the center of life is in the central nervous system, he proposes that life is everywhere in the organism, without a unique dominant centre. There is no central command as demonstrated by the death of parts of the body without affecting the life of other body's parts. Life is in the cells, the centre of activity of the body. Nevertheless, he avoids discussing controversial aesthetic and moral issues; his position is materialistic. Other aspects noted in this Lecture are the use of information from international researchers, e.g., Robin from France and Goodsir from England; the comparison of Pathological Processes with embryonal development; the statement of the recognition that the 'centre' of the cell is the nucleus; and that everything goes around the cell.

The final six Lectures - XV to XX - address the Pathological Processes. In Lecture XV, Virchow makes reference to the following processes: 'mortification', 'necrosis', necrobiosis, induration, fatty degeneration, fatty infiltration, and fatty metamorphosis (a form of 'necrobiosis'). He includes the normal process of fat absorption, the passage of fat into the epithelial cells, and other alterations of the fatty tissue. Under the heading of fatty metamorphosis, he characterizes the atheromatous process.

Virchow introduces Lecture XVI by circulating in the audience some gross specimens and describing the gross appearances of 'fatty degeneration' of the heart and distinguishing it from 'obesity of the heart' in which no muscle is identified grossly. He uses the terms fatty degeneration and fatty metamorphosis undistinguishable. He also brought cadavers for demonstration and carefully correlated gross with microscopic findings, setting the manner in which pathology should be academically practiced. According to Virchow, since Pathological Process are always similar, he recommends to know not only the location but also to observe their several stages since they are of long or short duration. Following his recommendation, he describes the successive stages on the evolution of cloudy swelling, fatty metamorphosis, fatty detritus (debris), and atrophy. Cloudy swelling precedes fatty degeneration. He stresses that these observations should not be based on clinical observations because they can be misleading. In particular, Virchow describes and explains the formation of an atheroma using gross specimens, microscopy, and experimental procedures to identify its components. In its formation at the wall of an artery, he recognizes two kinds of metamorphosis, fatty metamorphosis and atheromatous degeneration, being only the second preceded by inflammation as cause. In this description, there is a sense of continuity of the process based on the morphological description of the depot. Speculation is minimal. His theory of atheroma formation contrasts with that of Rokitansky.

In Lecture XVII Virchow introduces two Pathological Processes, 'amyloid change' ('lardaceous' and 'waxy' degeneration) and 'inflammation'. He describes the presence of amyloid by adding iodine and observing the result with the naked eye, exemplified by staining the branches of the hepatic artery and the central portions of the acini. After iodine, he adds sulphuric acid, considering the iodine-sulphuric test necessary for the diagnosis of amyloidosis. At all times, he emphasizes changes at the cellular level. In his investigation of the blood as the source of amyloid, Virchow mentions a 'physician from Toronto in Canada' who described some pale bodies in the blood of a patient with epilepsy. He denies the validity of the finding and considers it an error of observation. Virchow regards inflammation a Pathological Process resulting from 'irritation'. He excludes hyperaemia as the cause of inflammation. It is irritation that provokes a lesion in the cells, and it is their reaction that is responsible for the vascular response. Such response explains the formation of an exudate. Based on two kinds of exudation, he classifies inflammation into 'parenchymatous' and 'exudative'. The first is the product of trans-vascular fluid without tissue destruction and the second the manifestation of tissue destruction. In exudative inflammation, he includes fibrinous and mucous inflammation. These statements fall short of giving an explanation for the phenomenon, something that will be accomplished a few years later by his student Cohnheim.

Lectures XVIII, XIX, and XX are about new formations. According to Virchow, new formations originate by simple division and by the endogenous growth of cells. He proposes that the simple division ends in hypertrophy/hyperplasiae but that the endogenous growth of cells has three possible ends: an analogous structure (rare), a heterologous structure, and an intermediate stage in which the cell contains many nuclei. In Lecture XVIII, Virchow presents a correlation between embryology and pathology. He also introduces the Pathologic Process of 'tubercle' and gives a final blow to the blastema doctrine championed by the Vienna School by substituting it with the cell theory. Virchow insists that the blastema is no more than connective tissue containing cells. He uses the bones to illustrate his point. Bone formation had been explained before by Clopton Havers (1657-1702) and Duhamel using the blastema theory, but this is discredited by Virchow who, using the cellular theory, demonstrates that the medullary tissue is a type of connective tissue. As demonstrated with the microscope, he concludes that the tubercles arise from cells existent in the connective tissue. From his research on the tubercle, he attributes the origin of tumors (pathological new-formations) to a formative irritation, no different than inflammation. For him, cancer cells arise from normal (bone) cells.

In Lecture XIX, Virchow keeps the close association between infections and tumors. He classifies new formations into homologous and heterologous depending on the degree of similarity of the cell of origin and, therefore, tissue of origin (histogenesis). In his conception, heterologous new formations are destructive while homologous are only destructive under special circumstances. Based on this notion, Virchow considers that if an inflammatory process is destructive, it is, by definition, a heterologous formation no different from neoplasia. He uses catarrh, a form of inflammation, as an illustration of heterologous new formation. He mentions the 'fibrous or fibroid' of the uterus as an example of homologous new formation because it has the same structure as that of the walls of the 'hypertrophied' uterus. Like inflammation, a tumor is made of cells in constant reproduction because they do not last as long as the life of a tumor. Inflammation or neoplasia is the result of only the different nature of the stimulus. At no moment in this or other lectures, did he leave out his emphasis on the cell. For some of the descriptions, he referenced his papers published in *Archiv f. path. Anat.*

Lecture XX is also dedicated to heterologous new formations. It includes neoplasms and the tubercles. Virchow concludes that all new formations arise in cells of the connective tissue and that the lymphoid cells are the likely source for the origin of a tubercle. He discusses the terminology of these formations and introduces the term 'cheese metamorphosis'. Virchow considers that the production of fluid by a tumor gives its malignant character, the possibility to invade the surrounding tissues, and the capacity to metastasize.

At the end of Lecture XX, he states, "I have in the course of these lectures, gentlemen, developed to you as completely as it was possible for me here to do, the principles by means of which alone it is, according to my experience, possible to come to any correct decision in the case of Pathological Processes" (Virchow [1860] 1978, 488). Evidently, he is conscious about the relevance of his presentation. Based on a careful analysis of the text, it can be inferred that he is referring to the introduction of the term Pathological Processes and/or Pathological Reactions instead of Bichat's 'Morbid Reactions'; that the Processes occur at the cellular level as variations of the normal and resulting from injury; and that they would create another conceptualization of disease.

8.3 *Conclusions*

Cellular Pathology is the synthesis of Virchow's contribution to the origin of modern AP. The contribution is not reducible to the cell theory only. A careful analysis of the text indicates other topics, such as experimentation, anatomoclinical correlation, systematic use of the light microscope, and experimental identity of the Pathological Processes. This is the synthesis of the knowledge encountered in his lectures, knowledge that made possible the beginnings of modern (cellular) AP.

8.4 *The Legacy of Virchow's Cellular Pathology*

By the middle of the nineteenth century, the conditions were set for the beginnings of 'cellular pathology' as envisioned by Virchow in his lectures. Yet, his contribution did not come from nowhere. He built it upon the previous approaches to the knowledge of disease by Morgagni and Baillie and supplemented by the current investigation of many others. Future investigators followed Virchow's lead by applying new technology and new experimental designs. Virchow envisioned cellular pathology as:

• A change on the 'focus of attention' of morbid anatomy from organ/tissue to the cell, including the necessary methodology to study the new focus.

• The cell is the final site of disease.

• The bases to developing basic and clinical pathology.

• Acceptance that knowledge in pathology must rest on anatomy, histology, and physiology.

• Based on the microscope as an indispensable instrument in the new pathology.

• The end of long-standing principles like vitalism, humoralism, and dyscrasias and the acceptance of a new conceptualization of the nature of disease.

• The explanation of function by morphology.

• The kind of reasoning to be followed to approach experimentation in AP.

• An approach to study the Pathological Processes focusing on the cell.

• Anatomoclinical correlation taking into consideration the Pathological Processes.

• The incorporation of ancillary knowledge obtained from other sciences into AP.

CHAPTER 9

BASIC TECHNOLOGY

Interpreting the role of technology in the history of AP demands a previous discussion of the terms 'science' and 'technique' and admission that both require 'systematic scientific knowledge' as a prerequisite (Cardwell 2001, 449). In relation to science, it has been considered that technology is science-dependent and science is technology-dependent (Cardwell 2001, 4). Canguilhem adds, "not as two types of activity, one of which is grafted onto the other, but as two types of activity, each of which borrows from the other sometimes its solutions, sometimes its problems. ..." (Canguilhem 2008, 95). They are, then, complementary (Howell 1995). Although the distinction became blurred in the twentieth century, another interesting difference has been made by Mukherjee, "science understands nature; technology controls it" (Mukherjee 2011, 462). In relation to technique, it is considered an invention made possible because it is based on scientific knowledge (Cardwell 2001, 4). The New Lexicon Webster's Encyclopedic Dictionary of the English Language, Canadian Edition, defines technique as, "The entire body of procedures and methods of a science, art or craft." These inventions, procedures, and methods (i.e., techniques) – usually referred to us as technology – have

88

determined the contribution of technology to the history of AP.

In AP, the techniques utilized are many and vary according to the hypothesis to be tested. Some have subsisted with addition of new ones, whereas others disappeared and replaced by ones that are more effective. Without them, the Pathological Processes could not have been properly identified. In particular, microscopy and histochemistry with all their modifications have opened the opportunity to study the several levels of biological observation, that is, organ, tissue, and cell. Given their fundamental contributions, in particular to the practice of the specialty, the history of microscopy and histochemistry are the subject of our literature review.

9.1 *Microscopy*

In AP, the term 'microscopy' embraces a series of instruments that have in common an extension of the sense of sight with the intention to create patterns that would offer information on basic and systemic pathology. The science behind microscopy has allowed the invention of several types of instruments. Two kinds have been used extensively: the optical and the electron microscope. Both instruments have limitations that have been properly addressed in order to improve its yield, resulting in a variety of added devices designed for specific purposes.

Galileo Galilei is credited with the invention of the optical microscope as a modified telescope. Magnifying glasses, the precursor of the microscope, had been used before (Croft 2006, 5, 105). But it was Jan Leeuwenhoek from Delft, Holland, and Robert Hooke from London, England, who made the first documented observations with the instrument. In particular, Hooke's *Micrographia*, published in 1667, deserves special consideration given its transcendental contribution (Hooke 1667). The book is a record of his research on microscopy. In the preface, the author gives evidence that he was not just playing with the instrument, but using it as an extension of sighting. His intention was to improve his vision in order to collect better information for use in the scientific method as introduced by the Royal Society, the mechanical, the experimental, as he called it. He confronted the technical limitations of the compound instrument: glasses were not elliptical (convex); magnification, he states, "was only 1000 X" (sic); and objects appeared dark and indistinct because of small apertures. He complained that the instruments were not of optimal quality because they were made in England. Notwithstanding, he reported on modifications of the instrument on his extensive experimentation in plants and little animals with the intention to improve its limitations. He described three kinds of common images observed under examination: small bodies, small pores, and small motions. In 1658, at the same time of Hooke's studies, Athanasius Kircher (1602-1680), a Jesuit priest in Rome, published *Scrutinium pestis* in which he described the microscopic observations on decaying matter using an instrument with a 32X capacity (Garrison 1929, 545-252). Marcello Malpighi in Bologna was also doing the same studies using the same kind of instrument.

Leeuwenhoek used the simple (one lens) and Hooke the compound (two lenses) microscope. The inventors of the latter were Hans and Zacharias Jansen from Holland at the end of the sixteenth century (Croft 2006, 69-90). These instruments were rudimentary; Leeuwenhoek's microscope obtained a magnification with the range of 69 to 166 X (Snyder 2015, 55-56). Among other things, they suffered from two limitations, the spherical and the chromatic aberration. The first was the result of the lens and the second of the source of light. Spherical aberration is caused by the different focuses produced by the ray of light when hitting the periphery of convex lenses. It creates distorted shapes of the image. In chromatic aberration, the rays hit the surface of the lens and each one produces a different focus that is manifested in color fringes around the image. Small structures appear as globules, single or in chains. It is the results of the nature of the white light that is the product of a combination of the whole spectrum of colors. The first achromatic compound microscope to correct this aberration was designed in Paris in 1824 (Ewing 1940, 3, 5; King 1982, 36). The correction of the chromatic aberration is also attributed to Joseph Jackson Lister (1786-1860) in 1830 (Garrison 1931, 408). Giambatista Amici (1786-1863) also improved the achromatic lens and invented the immersion lens in 1850 (Castiglioni 1941, 675). The systematic introduction of the light microscope in AP is attributed to Virchow. The importance of the microscope in this science and related fields was also promoted by some of Müller's students, in particular Jacob Henle (1809-1885), and Albert von Kolliker (1817-1905) (Porter 1999, 321).

The use of the optical microscope requires properly processed tissue to make acceptable observations. The first preparations were taken from gross specimens; Malpighi described pouring them with ink. Small pieces of fresh tissue obtained by cutting with a razor blade were squeezed between two slides and followed by treatment with acetic acid and ether to eliminate debris and fat (King 1982, 36). These existent crude procedures were eventually replaced by fixation, processing, and staining that initially produced unimaginable tissue distortion way far away from the image of a living tissue. It was the Czech Johannes Evangelista Purkinje (1787-1863) who introduced the microtome to replace tissue sectioning with razor blades and the balsam to prepare microscopic slides (Castiglioni 1941, 679). Proper tissue preparation for histological examination was achieved before the end of the nineteenth century when a proper fixation was accomplished in 1870, staining by 1880, and fixation with formalin by 1883 (Porter 1999, 321; Vollmer and Goldmann 2011).

A protocol that produced acceptable images for analysis already existed in 1881. Specimens could be examined while fresh or processed. When fresh, tissue was cut with a microtome or simply by breaking it into pieces with a needle; then it was put into sodium chloride or glycerine on a glass slide. When processed, tissue was first hardened with a solution of bichromate of potash (Miller's fluid), cut and sectioned, embedded in wax and olive oil, and stained with a solution of hæmatoxylin and alumen or carmine. Finally, if the specimen was preserved, it was mounted in glycerine or Dammar varnish (Green 1881, 334-340). Similar improved protocols have become standard and, therefore, comparable. It is important to remember that microscopic images are a static version of a cross-section in time of a process. They should not be used as referents to confirm dynamic sequences of a phenomenon.

Historically, techniques that modified the optical microscope followed the correction of the aberrations. Consequently, other types of microscopes were created; for example, there are dark field, phase contrast, polarizing, fluorescence, and confocal microscopes. In spite of the modifications, a fundamental limitation of the optical microscope continued being present, namely 'resolution' which is the visual capacity of the human eye to distinguish between two points in space. This normal capacity is between 0.1 to 0.2 mm. Resolution determines magnification; the better the resolution, the higher the magnification. This limitation was overcome by the electron microscope.

The electron microscope uses electrons as the source of light and magnets as lenses. By increasing resolution, the instrument augments the magnification to hundreds of thousands dependent upon the quality of the machine. There are two basic types of electron microscopes: the transmission (TEM) and the scanning (SEM) electron microscope. The theory behind their design was developed by Ernst Karl Abbe (1840-1905) and Louis Victor Pierre Raymond, 7th Duc de Broglie (1892-1987). Based on their theory and the development of the cathode ray oscilloscope, Ernst August Friedrich Ruska (1906-1988) and Max Knoll (1897-1969) built the first TEM in Germany in 1931 (Peven and Gruhn 1985, 683-691; Erlandson 1987, 487-505). James Hillier

(1915-2007) and Albert Prebus (1913-1997) built the first instrument in North America in 1938. The functional components of a TEM (source of electrons and magnets) correspond to the same parts of an optical microscope in an inverted position. The principles - not the reagents - of fixation, processing, and tissue staining are the same as in tissue preparation for light microscopy. The end result is the staining of membranes, organelles, and intra and extracellular material, which are the components hit by the electrons (Weakley 1981). In the case of SEM, a coat of gold is added to cover the surface of the specimen. As its name indicate, the instrument is a scanning machine no different than a fax device. The electrons impinge on the surface of the specimen and then collected, providing the observer with a tridimensional image. This type of microscope is useful in experimentation but of limited use in diagnosis.

9.2 *Histochemistry*

The beginning of histochemistry is traced to the eighteenth century. Leeuwenhock described the use of a dye – saffron – to stain muscle fibres for the first time in a letter to the Royal Society in 1714 that was not published until five years later. To that report, it followed others on the use of biological stains for microscopic examination (Conn 1953, 10-11). However, it is François-Vincent Raspail (1794-1878) - a botanist - who is considered the founder of histochemistry. Although he did not introduce the stain, Raspail's merit rests on his extensive use of the iodine reaction to identify starch with the microscope and his publication of two books on the subject in 1830 and 1833. He was not a morphologist (Pearse 1953).

The application of chemistry to the analysis of tissues in AP is as old as the Paris School of medicine in the first half of the nineteenth century. Laennec - a contemporary of Raspail - referred to chemistry as a method for studying the alterations that disease causes in tissues and as a complement to anatomical studies. He called it "pathological chemistry" and favoured it for its etiological considerations and therapeutic applications (Laennec 1884, 16-18). Following these beginnings, there was an explosion of the application of new stains at the middle of the century (Conn 1953, 10-11). These years coincided with Virchow's efforts to introduce systematically the use of the light microscope to study tissues/cells in AP.

The history of histochemistry is closely linked to the dye industry because the production of dyes for biological staining was a bi-product of the textile's needs to improve the colouring of cotton fabrics performed previously with archaic and inefficient technics (Cadwell 2001, 146). Before 1856, there were already stains for textiles extracted from plants, but the process was kept secret. The synthesis of murexide, an aniline dye, by William Henry Perkin (1838-1907) in London in 1856 revolutionized the technology for the production of dyes. The new technology became the future source of these chemicals for biological purposes. The revolution began in England and then Germany, the country that expanded the industry (Cardwell 2001, 297-300). In the 1880s, the Germans took the lead (Mukherjee 2011, 81-82).

Based on these considerations, histochemistry can be described as consisting of two overlapping branches, one dominated by the chemists and the other by the pathologists. The first considers histochemistry as the science that use dyes and other compounds to unravel the chemical nature of the tissue's components (Conn 1953, 13). It deals with dyes, their chemical composition, the nature of the stained tissue components and uses frozen tissue to be effective (Wick 2012, 71-78). The second is the branch that deals with the use of stains to identify tissue components processed and observed under the light microscope. Different from the chemist, the anatomical pathologist is concerned with the morphological appearances in tissue sections. This kind of staining became known as 'biological' and defined as, "a dye used for making microscopic object more clearly visible than they would be unstained" (Conn 1953, 7, 51-52). Histochemistry was then recognized as the application of dyes to identify particular tissues under the light microscope. Only a few authors were more interested in the chemical reaction of the dyes with tissue components in order to identity them (Pearse 1953, 8).

Since the very beginnings, the differential staining of the nucleus and the cytoplasm with Hematoxylin and Eosin (H&E) suggested the potential role of dyes. Other stains were directed to identify tissue/cell, connective tissue, and neurological tissues (Conn 1953, 11-12). Progressively, several new stains were introduced, for instance, aniline dyes by Bencke in 1862, hematoxylin by Heinrich Wilhelm Gottfried von Waldeyer-Hartz (1836-1921) in 1863, the methyl-violet for amyloid by Cornil in 1875, the Gram stain by Hans Christian Joachim Gram (1853-1938) in 1884, the peroxidase reaction by Brandenburg in 1900, and the identification of calcium by von Kóssa in 1901 (Pearse 1953, 4-7; Conn 1953, 10-11; Chan 2014, 12-32; Ortiz-Hidalgo and Pina-Oviedo 2018, 4-14). American and Canadian pathologists also made important contributions that overshadowed many of their European counterparts; such is the case of Frank Burr Mallory (1862-1941) in Boston and Claude L. Pierre Masson (1880-1959) in Montreal. Virchow used carmine as his preferred dye for staining microscopic sections. Other stains were developed to be used to identify micro-organisms. Dyes, however, have not been the only 'histochemical reagents' (Conn 1953, 5). Other materials, like silver, are also used. The famous drawings of the nervous systems by Santiago Ramon y Cajal (1852-1934) used a modification of the silver stain introduced by Golgi (*The Beautiful Brain* 2017). Currently, the application of special stains is becoming of limited use because new techniques have been introduced.

After 1980, with the exception of the H&E stain, only some of the stains are applied routinely (e.g., PAS, mucicarmine, and silver stain). The incorporation of tagged antibodies for morphological identification of tissue components and cells (immunohisto(cyto)chemistry) has exploded with the introduction of poly- and mono-clonal antibodies. The introduction of polyclonal antibodies was initiated using fluorescein-labelled antibodies, a technique introduced by Albert Coons (1912-1978) from Harvard in 1941 (Coons, Creech, and Jones 1941, 200-202). It was later followed by the use of enzymes. The introduction of monoclonal antibodies was the consequence of the production of these kind of antibodies by the Nobel laurates George Köhler (1946-1995) and Cesar Milstein (1927-2002) that, due to their specificity, replaced the use of polyclonal antibodies. The tagged antibody and/or an anti-antibody detect the reaction site if the antigen (a protein) is present. Immunohisto(cyto)chemistry is a morphological expression of cell function (Vollmer and Goldmann 2011). Later, molecular testing has made inroads into everyday practice.

9.3 *Conclusions*

After discussing the distinction between science, technology, and technique, the history of two fundamental techniques that are part of the practice of AP - microscopy and histochemistry - were explored. The chronological record of microscopy focused on the light and the electron microscope. The history of histochemistry followed the identification of two branches, one controlled by chemists and the other by pathologists. The latter has played a role on diagnosis and experimentation. Nevertheless, it has decreased in importance, being almost replaced by a technique that uses the same principles but other reagents, that is, immunohisto(cyto)chemistry. Our history ends in 1980, the time when light microscopy continues being the everlasting instrument in use and molecular pathology techniques opened the possibility of improvements in research and diagnosis in AP.

CHAPTER 10

CONTRIBUTORY BIOMEDICAL KNOWLEDGE

A science does not originate and develop in isolation. There is a symbiosis in the process in which one science contributes to the development of another. AP is not an exception. As an outcome of anatomy, AP inherited its morphological background. But once gained its own identity, AP became influenced by other sciences, most importantly, physiology, chemistry, bacteriology, and immunobiology. After 1980 one could add genetics. Reciprocally, AP has provided them with a morphological understanding of their experimental discoveries. The biomedical knowledge offered by these disciplines has been crucial for the origin, development, consolidation, and maturity of AP. A selected literature review of the history of these sciences reveals their influence on the evolution of pathologic knowledge.

The development of these sciences in the nineteenth and twentieth centuries has impacted pathologic knowledge directly (conceptually) and indirectly (cognitively). Conceptually, in the first half of the nineteenth century physiology and chemistry evolved into physiopathology and physiological chemistry, adding a dynamic (functional) interpretation to anatomic findings the first and qualitative and quantitative assessments of the functional changes the second. Eventually, physiological chemistry evolved into biochemistry, a science that unravels the physicochemical composition and functioning of the cell. Cognitively, in the second half of the same century bacteriology and its by-product – immunobiology - introduced two recognizable modalities of reasoning in AP. Bacteriology demonstrated, for the first- time, solid evidence of uni-causality of disease (i.e., cause-effect) by an independent etiologic agent. Immunobiology, on the other hand, modified the understanding of a 'body system' because its components (i.e., cells and organs), by not having an anatomic continuity, act all over the body when activated. This science also introduced immunohisto(cyto) chemistry, a technique that revolutionized laboratory medicine.

10.1 *Physiology/Physiopathology*

In the nineteenth century, Europe was the continent where experimentation applied to the study of anatomy evolved into a combination of structure and function, that is, physiology/physiopathology. This was the consequence of intellectual changes occurring at the turn of the century. Physiopathology had an impact on the reasoning of physicians dedicated to pathology, namely, the incorporation of function in the interpretation of anatomical findings. Two schools of thought dominated that transition, the Paris and the German Schools (Lesch

1984, 5-6; Malkin 1993, 107-127, 143-158). However, the schools differed on their interpretations of the same event.

In Paris and Germany, the terminology of physiology/physiopathology was not exactly identical. In France, François Magendie (1783-1855) defined 'human physiology' as the scientific basis of medicine (Lesch 1984, 174). For Claude Bernard (1813-1878), also from Paris, 'experimental medicine' consisted of physiology, pathology, and therapeutics (Bernard [1865] 1957, 1); stating as pathology the "knowledge of disease and of their determining causes" (Bernard [1865] 1957, 2). In Germany, Virchow considered experimental medicine the same as Bernard, but he called it 'scientific medicine' (Bonah 1998, 34). It consisted of pathology, that included abnormal physiology, and therapy. In both countries, therefore, one can infer that they were referring to normal and abnormal physiology applied to medicine.

The difference on terminology also influenced the conceptual understanding of the term 'pathology'. In Paris it was understood closer to physio-pathology due to its emphasis on physiology. In Germany, due to Virchow's contribution, it was understood as cellular pathology (Bonah 1998, 31-32). The difference may be due to the fact that in Germany AP and physiology were born independently (44).

In Paris, Magendie (1783-1885) and his student Bernard were the leading figures, although there were other clinician-pathologist-experimentalists (Castiglioni 1941, 680-684; Lesch 1984, 5-6). The transformation of a morphological evaluation of an autopsy to a physiopathological one was clearly established by

Bernard. He insisted on a post-mortem evaluation of the disappearance of the tissues' function because this may explain death rather than the morphological changes that are the late results of disease. He even labeled the approach a "physiological autopsy" (Bernard [1865] 1957, 157). In Germany, the contributions to physiopathology in the first half of the nineteenth century overlapped with that of the French. It was the universities' reform that introduced science into medicine, a reform epitomized by physiopathology (Sudhoff 1926, 363-374).

Conversion of thinking is always a multi-causal phenomenon. In the second half of the nineteenth century, the incorporation of function to anatomic thinking by the French and Germans was enhanced by the introduction of the cell theory since physiology/physiopathology alone did not answer all questions. The conversion is found in Virchow's *Cellular Pathology* and in his student Cohnheim's *Lectures on General Pathology* (Cohnheim 1889). They illustrated explanations based on experimentation and its role in physiology/physiopathology, the participation of the cell theory, and a functional pattern of reasoning. Concurrent with these events, researchers in this field began to turn their attention to the whole body (e.g., digestion, internal milieu, respiration) instead of organs as had been dominant when anatomy was the prevalent science (Singer and Underwood 1962, 236).

10.2 *Physiological Chemistry/Biochemistry*

Simple chemical procedures applied to urine and blood were introduced into medicine in the late seventeenth century by Thomas Willis and Robert Boyle (1627-1691). One century later, William Hewson and William Cruikshank of the Hunter School in London did the same to blood (Cruikshank 1786; Hewson 1774). These applications were interpreted according to humouralism, but the chemical analysis of tissues explained by solidism was more difficult to obtain. As a consequence, the interest in the chemical analysis of fluids to answer many clinical questions was revived in the 1830s and 1840s (Reiser 1981, 122-128).

The chemical analysis of the body's tissues and fluids became known as physiological chemistry; that is, chemistry as a measurement of physiological processes. It offered an extension of the functional thinking initiated by physiology/physiopathology by assessing qualitatively and quantitatively the dynamic changes observed experimentally. Physiological chemistry eventually developed into an independent science that would transform into biochemistry in the twentieth century.

The history of physiological chemistry can be traced to German researchers. They discovered many chemical compounds in body fluids and, very importantly, introduced the concept of metabolism. These studies were also performed in Paris (Ackerknecht 1982, 151, 165). Physiological chemistry expanded further to research on the digestion of food. In North America, William Beaumont (1785-1853), a surgeon in the American Army, studied, by accident, a gastric fistula in the Canadian Alexis Saint Martin and described the nature of the gastric juice and gastric digestion (Beaumont [1833] 1959).

In the twentieth century, physiological chemistry, now as biochemistry, became characterized by studies on nutrition, vitamins, hormones, enzymes, and metabolism; that is, whole body studies with emphasis at the cellular level. After WWII, advances in genetics joined biochemistry to be transformed into molecular biology. The nature of the biochemical research favored the development of a pattern of reasoning for pathologists, namely bio-feed-back, a dynamic cause-effect integration as illustrated in the intracellular metabolic pathways.

10.3 *Bacteriology*

Bacteriology introduced the concept of uni-causality in disease, influencing the reasoning process of pathologists. Its impact was so remarkable that its name was incorporated in the designation of universities' pathology departments; they became 'Department of Pathology and Bacteriology'. Its importance is connected to the role that pathologic knowledge has on the study of disease. Before bacteriology, there were diverse opinions about the transmission of disease: contagion, miasma, putrefaction, fermentation, and spontaneous generation. These terms explained the transmission of disease but they were completely non-specific (Porter 1999, 428-430). By the last quarter of the nineteenth century, several lines of experimental research discredited these theories and enlightened the specificity of disease transmission.

The main proponents of the new theories were the French Louis Pasteur (1822-1895) and the German Heinrich Hermann Robert Koch (1843-1910). Pasteur's contributions can be summarized in his experimental investigations on fermentation, putrefaction, spontaneous generation, and vaccination (Porter 1999, 431-437). Koch sets bacteriology on a solid basis and also related it to pathologic knowledge. He did the latter by creating the technology necessary for the culture of bacteria. In addition to the discovery of the tuberculous and cholera bacilli, he is also considered the author of the postulates that determine the necessary conditions to consider an agent the cause of disease. In this, he followed the lead introduced years before by his teacher Henle (King 1971, 257-269; Reiser 1981, 141; Ackerknecht 1982, 179).

It was the incontrovertible demonstration of micro-organisms in the second half of the nineteenth century that left no doubt about their cause of specific diseases. Although several fungi and parasites (Trichomonas vaginalis in 1837) were described in the first half of the nineteenth century, the period of discovery extended from 1849, when the anthrax bacillus was identified, to 1906 when the organism responsible for pertussis was discovered. Curiously, between 1879 and 1900, twenty-one years, twenty-one microorganisms were identified (Singer and Underwood 1962, 390-391; Ackerknecht 1982, 176). Studies on the cause extended knowledge to the mechanism of action of these agents and the immediate response by the host (Sigerist 1932, 207; Ackerknecht 1982,180; Porter 1999, 442). Finally, the history of the discovery of viruses is the history of a filtrate free of cells. (Porter 1999, 458-459). Concomitantly with these discoveries, the response of the host to the presence of bacteria led to the origin of a new science that also influenced AP, namely immunobiology.

10.4 *Immunobiology*

The history of immunobiology may be confusing given the variety of topics involved, the names of its numerous contributors, explosion in the number of terms, and its lack of distinction from hypersensitivity (Anderson 1971, 542). However, this history is important because it changed the concept of the body's system by pathologists from the classical one consisting of the anatomical continuity of organs to one represented by cells with its products and organs dispersed in the whole body. Its generated knowledge also contributed by introducing new techniques, in particular immunohisto(cyto)chemistry, that has played a crucial role for the development of techniques in molecular pathology.

The knowledge of the body's immunity is old. Its history dates back to the ancient cultures of the Far East and Roman times when it was closely related to the body's response to infection. In the eighteenth century, Edward Jenner's production of the small-pox vaccine received particular attention (Anderson 1971, 543). In spite of the practical utility of these advances, these discoveries were not accompanied by rational explanations about their mechanisms of production. It is not until the last quarter of the nineteenth century when explanations began to appear and the modern history of immunity can start to be traced (Oertel 1927, 114-118). The beginning of knowledge on the body's immunity is attributed to

Pasteur and Koch, followed by the identification of two fundamental elements in the theory of immunity referred to as toxins and anti-toxins at the time. By 1900, three hallmark discoveries were already present: a theory of immunity, the role of serum in the body's defense, and vaccination (Porter 1999, 589). From here, two lines of research followed: the humoral and the cellular. It is along these two lines that the history of immunobiology can be studied in the twentieth century.

The basic conception of *humoral immunity* is based on substances present in blood to which are given the name of "antibodies" reacting against agents labelled "antigens." By the 1900s, three theories were postulated for the mechanism of an antigen-antibody reaction. The first was chemical, an enzymatic reaction; the second was based on the physicochemical properties of the reagents, a form of precipitation as postulated by Karl Landsteiner (1868-1943); and the third was through cell receptors as advanced in the 'side-chain theory' of the German Paul Ehrlich (Porter 1999, 590). Ehrlich's theory, the most popular, proposed that the toxin attaches to the cell protoplasm through a molecule that is surrounded by several receptors that he called side-chains. The end result is the destruction of the cell and the liberation of the complex toxin/side-chain into the blood. If the cell survives, it replaces the new receptor and, if they are produced in abundance, they could be joined to a toxin present in the blood before reaching the target cells (Oertel 1927, 152-153; Singer and Underwood 1962, 413). The theory was unacceptable because it did not explain the response to a multitude of antigens.

In the 1950s, MacFarlane Burnet (1899-1985) modified the 'natural selection' theory of the Dane Niels Kaj Jerne (1911-1994), bringing back Ehrlich's side-chain theory under the name of "clonal selection theory." According to Burnet, antibodies are a cell's product located on its surface as receptors. When exposed to an antigen, the antigen attaches to the receptor. The information to produce antibodies already exists in immunocompetent cells, and it is the antigen that triggers the proliferation of these cells at their encounter (Mazumdar 1989, 5).

The identification of the nature of the antibodies had to wait until the development of successive techniques. In the middle of the nineteenth century, plasma proteins were separated into albumin and globulin. Yet, it was not until 1938 that Tiselius and Kabat identified antibodies as gamma-globulins (Moulin 1989, 293). For the intimate identification of antibodies, two techniques had to be designed. The first was serum electrophoresis by Karl Landsteiner (1868-1943) and Wolfgang Pauli in Vienna and the ultra-centrifugal separation by sedimentation by Theodor Svedberg (1884-1971) in Sweden. To these techniques it followed the use of papain digestion and chromatography. Using them, Rodney Porter (1917-1985) in London was able to divide the globulin into two fractions, the Fab and the Fc fragments. Further methods using the 7S globulin of Svedberg divided the component into a heavy and a light chain (Mazumdar 1989, 7-8). The result of the application of this technology was necessary to make sense of the use of immunohisto(cyto)chemistry and poly- and mono-clonal antibodies in AP in the following years. Another important participant within the field of the humoral immunity was "Complement," so called by Ehrlich (Gladstone and Abraham 1970, 1026).

The humoral theory of immune response was defended by the Germans - following Ehrlich's contributions - by postulating that bacteria acted through the production of toxins and the resulting body's defense mechanism by producing anti-toxins. The French, otherwise, proposed that the mechanism of defense was the result of the cellular activity of phagocytosis by macrophages. This proposal, the so-called *"cellular theory,"* was put forward at the end of the nineteenth century by Metchnikoff as an alternative explanation (Metchnikoff [1891] 1968, 33). These cells have received several names according to their function or origin, such as histiocytes, clasmatocytes, polyblasts, reticulum cells, and reticular cells (Vernon-Roberts 1972, 1-2).

In 1924, Aschoff introduced the term "Reticuloendothelial System" referring to body cells that take up vital stains. Using this technique, he demonstrated that these cells had a common function of phagocytosis and corresponded to the cells described by Metchnikoff. He used the term "reticuloendothelial" because was believed that the cells lining the sinuses (endothelial) present in the liver, spleen, bone marrow, and lymph nodes were responsible for the production of the fibrils (reticular) that support the sinuses (Vernon-Roberts 1972, 1-2). The history of humoral and cellular immunities, however, is incomplete without considering the role played by the *T-cells* and *soluble factors.*

The history of T-cells started with the discovery of the tuberculin reaction by Koch in the early 1890s, although it was until the 1960s that the role of the thymus and lymphocytes became clear (Mazumdar 1989, 9). Thymic cells, called 'T' cells, were necessary (help) for the response to occur. T cells were later demonstrated to be a heterogenous population that performed the function of help, suppress, and kill cells (Waksman 1989, 148-149; Porter 1999, 593).

For both types of immune response to occur, they need the assistance of *'soluble factors'*. In the decade of the 1960s, a series of factors, with names such as macrophage chemotactic factor and interferon, were isolated. At the end of the decade, the name "lymphokines" was given to this family of mediators of immunity (Lawrence 1989, 222-224).

In the 1970s, several important developments were reported: the close participation in the immune response by B and T lymphocytes, macrophages, and other cell types such as basophil/mast cells, eosinophils, and polymorphs; the existence of a mucosal type of immune response; and the 'antibody-dependent cell-mediated cytotoxicity' (Waskman 1989, 149-154). The number of soluble factors also expanded. The complexity of the immune response mediated by cells dispersed all over the body and their products contributed to new conceptualizations and patterns of reasoning by pathologists.

10.5 *Conclusions*

Contributory biomedical knowledge generated in the nineteenth and twentieth century directly impacted pathologic knowledge. This impact modified concepts and the scientific reasoning of pathologists. Our focus of attention has been on physiology, chemistry, bacteriology, and immunobiology. Each impacted AP differently. Physiology gave a dynamic (functional) interpretation to findings from a static observation of structures. Biochemistry introduced a systematic study of the intimate nature of the body tissue's components. Bacteriology brought causality to the forefront of AP. Immunobiology changed not only the appreciation of body's systems from a localized to a diffuse location but also contributed new technologies. In the future, the participation of genetics will need to be incorporated.

PART II: PATHOLOGIC KNOWLEDGE

CHAPTER 11

WHAT IS PATHOLOGIC KNOWLEDGE?

AP is a science whose methodologies are used to obtain an end-product that is called 'pathologic knowledge', the essence of the specialty. In AP the foundational knowledge – the basic – is known as Pathological Processes, so named by Virchow. Each Process is here considered a 'unit' of knowledge for purpose of evaluation.

The term 'knowledge' has several conceptual interpretations (Himsworth 1970; McNeely and Wolverton 2008; Nagel 2014; Sosa 2017). In the academic discipline of history, terms like 'knowledge' are rarely defined, leaving the reader to understand the meaning of terms. McGill University historian Don Bates' unsuccessful life project was to find a proper definition of 'scientific knowledge' (Bates 2009, 23-84). Lack of a definition, however, should not prevent us from pondering over the possibility of having a working understanding of pathologic knowledge and its relation to scientific knowledge. Once this is settled, it is possible to conclude that pathologic knowledge is a variant of the scientific. This conclusion can be uncovered in an evaluation of its foundational component; namely, the Pathological Processes.

11.1 *Understanding "Scientific Knowledge"*

In the literature, the terms 'science', 'scientific method', and 'knowledge' are closely related, actually considered equivalent. Some authors even categorically affirm that "science is the scientific method itself" (Klemke et al. 1998, 34, 51). It follows that knowledge in the sciences would be considered an end product generated by the scientific method.

Using the scientific method, knowledge is produced experimentally through a complex empiric-rational process that comprises matters of facts, perception, and mentalities. 'Matters of facts' are objective and verifiable observations using nature and laboratory experiments (Collingwood 1994, 170). The facts are evidence notwithstanding that this evidence, in a substantial majority of times, is temporal because it will be modified according to new hypotheses, new technology, and other ways of knowing. Facts are the empirical information on which perception is based and reasoning is founded (Shapin and Schaffer 1985, 22-23, 67). 'Perception' is the handling and interpretation of those facts using reasoning. It refers only to sensory perceptions, with or without the aid of technology. 'Mentalities' are the end-result of the production of knowledge and the one shared by a scientific community. It is the knowledge itself. Mentalities are based on the empirical findings, but also on the interaction of perception, experience, and the conceptualizations in which a scientific group has developed. The rational component of mentalities participates in factual observation since observation is theory-driven (Brown 1987, v-ix).

Scientific knowledge is classified from several points of view. It can be concrete and abstract, with the concrete being organic and inorganic (Pearson 1900, 514-527). It is also classified into basic and applied based on attributes; that is, basic knowledge has the characteristics obtained by laboratory experimentation, whereas applied has those of nature-experiments. Scientific knowledge is also considered non-specialized (non-expert) and specialized (expert) (Himsworth 1970, 15-20, 52-53). The non-expert, as its name implies, is knowledge communicated in common language to an educated general public. Expert knowledge demands a level of subject matter mastery obtained through an educational process to understand it. Hence, readers of research reports must be experts to understand them (Temkin 1977, 34). Pathologic knowledge is a variant of the expert.

11.2 *Understanding "Pathologic Knowledge"*

What pathologists study when becoming experts, and the source of their professional practice, is scientific knowledge. Based on these considerations, I understand – not define – 'pathologic knowledge' as collected mental information, concrete and abstract, obtained by the observation-experimentation of disease, supported by experience, consensually accepted by the community of pathologists, and applied to problem solving situations. It fulfills the criteria that characterize scientific knowledge;

that is, it is factual, rational, analytic, specialized, verifiable, systematic, and explanatory (Bunge n.d., 16-36). Its identity is strongly influenced by the dichotomy "normal versus pathological."

Pathologic knowledge can be obtained from existent bank of data (textbooks, other literature, internet, etc.) and rests upon previous knowledge and the existing opinion of pathologists. It is perfected by learning skills and experience. Pathologists use this knowledge to reinforce their laboratory and clinical experiences, to address problem—solving situations, to critically assess current opinion and literature, to apply to new cases, and to contribute during interactions with colleagues and clinicians.

The 'foundational' pathologic knowledge consists of a group of Processes that have evolved historically through observation and experimentation. They are the basic manifestations of pathologic knowledge. Each of these Processes is considered a 'unit of knowledge' as found in the basic science section of pathology textbooks. The units are brought into existence by observations with naked eye of gross specimens and by the application of light microscopy to the corresponding tissues and cells samples. Knowledge so obtained is refined using animal models, through incorporating specific ancillary techniques (e.g., histochemistry, immunohisto(cyto)chemistry, electron microscopy, in-situ hybridization), and by correlating findings with clinical data. Up to the last quarter of the twentieth century, data was solely generated by studying phenotypes. Later, added information begun to be obtained from genotypes using molecular testing.

In brief, the foundational manifestation of pathologic knowledge is a form of scientific knowledge expressed in units. The units correspond to the morbid modifications of the organs, tissues, and cells due to disease and are known as "Pathological Processes," a term introduced by Virchow (Virchow [1860] 1978, ix, 279; Welch [1897] 1937, 248-310). Other names that refer to the same reactions are Bichat's "morbid symptoms" (Bichat [1824] 2010, 23), Adami's "morbid and reactive processes" (Adami 1908, 373-374), Sigerist's "pathological reactions" (Sigerist 1932, 129-149), and Anderson's "fundamental results of injury to tissues" (Anderson 1971, 37).

CHAPTER 12

THE PATHOLOGICAL PROCESSES

The Pathological Processes are the basic reactions of the body to injury; the essence of pathologic knowledge, its foundational component; and belong to the area of expertise of anatomic pathologists (Foucault 1994, 124-140). For this reason, a history of their conceptual evolution under the context of morphology becomes relevant. This visualization is enhanced by having an understanding of their inception by X. Bichat at the dawn of the nineteenth century. This formulation was followed by Virchow's expanded analysis at the middle of that century and by the introduction of new concepts, research, and technology in the following years. This scenario would set the basis for the future direction of pathologic knowledge in the twenty and twenty-first century, in particular through the influence of genetics.

The conceptual understanding of the basic reactions of the body to injury was introduced by X. Bichat in his *General Anatomy*, a pathophysiology textbook influenced by vitalism. He called them "Morbid Symptoms" and classified under one of the four body's vital properties. In his classification, the symptoms were due to alterations on the 'organic sensibility and insensible contractility in health' of the solid component of the body. The other three vital properties were responsible for functional, not anatomical, alterations in disease; such as pain, diarrhea, and convulsions (Bichat [1824] 2010, 2-10, 23-24, 32). Bichat listed six Morbid Symptoms: inflammation, formation of pus, scirrhus, hemorrhage, increase or suppression of secretions and exhalations, and imperfect nutrition producing tumors and cysts (Bichat [1824] 2010, 23). This conceptualization was further modified by Laennec.

Laennec developed a theory of morbid lesions in a manner that Bichat never did, but he never finished this work. In 1804, he created a classification of the reactions that were published in the *Journal of Corvisart* and the *Dictionary of Medical Sciences* (Laennec 1884, xi). These publications have been analyzed and contextualized by Duffin and Maulitz (Maulitz 1987, 76-77; Duffin 1998, 61-67, 260, 267). It was not until 1884 that Laennec's nephew Mériadec Laennec and Victor André Cornil (1837-1908) collected the information and published it, leaving the preface, the classification of the tissue and organic lesions, and the chapters as originally written by Laennec (Laennec 1884, vi).

Laennec thought that the knowledge of disease could be reduced to five areas: causes, body alterations, altered functions, course and prevention, and treatment. He established that the first three are the areas in which AP could contribute (Laennec 1884, 19-20). Laennec proposed five alterations in the body's organs that correspond to tissue derangements: alterations of texture, form, nutrition, position, and presence of foreign bodies

(53-54). The one relevant to our theme is 'alterations of texture' (i.e., tissues). Their causes were three: accidental development of one tissue or matter (e.g., tuberculous matter; cancer), accumulation or extravasation of a body fluid (anasarca), and dissolution of continuity in an organ (wounds and fractures) (60). The accidental development of tissues or matter was of two orders: tissues similar to natural tissues and those noted only in cases of disease. The first order consisted of ossification and degenerations (62); the second included inflammation, tubercles, scirrhus, gelatinous degenerations or gumma, cerebriform degenerations, melanosis, sclerosis, cirrhosis, and other kinds of degenerations (63-64). Laennec continued making an extensive description and analysis of each one of them and their effect on the organ and on the whole-body's economy. These ideas were developed further by Virchow in his Lectures.

In *Cellular Pathology*, Virchow called attention to the cell as the site of the pathological reactions, used the term "Pathological Processes" and "Morbid Processes" instead of Morbid Symptoms, and considered inflammation the final pathway of these processes (Virchow [1860] 1978, ix, 279). In Lectures II and III, he unveiled previous beliefs on the intimate nature of the body; that is, fibres and globules, theories that, according to him, interfere with the explanation of the Processes. In Lecture III, Virchow redefined terms like hypertrophy, hyperplasia, progressive (fatty) atrophy, and fatty degeneration. He defined hypertrophy as, "… those cases in which the individual elements of a structure take up a considerable amount of matter, and thereby become larger; and in which, in consequence of the simultaneous enlargement of a number of elements, at last the whole of an organ may become swollen" (65). Virchow described two types of hypertrophy: simple and numerical, the latter meaning an increase in the number of cells (66). He also defines hyperplasia as, "… an enlargement takes place in consequence of an increase in the number of the elements" (65). He did not define progressive (fatty) atrophy but explained its morphology in skeletal muscle and in the description of an artery introduces the term "fatty degeneration", only stating that a layer of it is replaced by "masses of fat-granules." In Lecture X, Virchow introduced the concept of thrombosis, embolism, and metastatic deposits. He defined thrombosis as, "a real coagulation of the blood at a certain fixed spot." His definition had the intention of proving that Cruveilhier's phlebitis theory was wrong (199). Cruveilhier had postulated that inflammation of a vein was the initial lesion and the intravascular formation of a clot was its consequence. Virchow also introduced the term 'embolia' and defined it as, "the detachment of larger or smaller fragments from the end of the softening thrombus which are carried along by the current of blood and driven into remote vessels" (204). In Lecture XIV, he dealt with cell irritation, giving as examples hypertrophy, inflammation, and cloudy swelling (295-297). Virchow described cloudy swelling without mentioning that he was the first to describe this process (296-297). Fig. 98 of this Lecture gives the impression that in renal tubules cloudy swelling is followed by fatty metamorphosis and disintegration (296).

The final six lectures, XV to XX, directly address the Pathological Processes. In Lecture XV, Virchow divided the Processes into 'active' and 'passive', depending on the manifestation of activity, or lack of, by the involved cells when responding to an external injury. After defining passive processes, he divided them into necrobiosis and degeneration (Virchow [1860] 1978, 316-319). The term 'necrobiosis' had been introduced before by K. H. Schultz to refer to disease in general, but Virchow restricted the term to cell destruction as a result of a Pathological Process. He defined necrobiosis as, "... death brought on by (altered) life – a spontaneous wearing out of living parts – the destruction and annihilation consequent upon life – natural as opposed to violent death (mortification)." Necrobiosis ends in 'softening' (318). In these definitions, he mixed histological observations with gross findings. On the other hand, passive processes in which cells diminish their power and end up destroyed were called 'degeneration'. Nevertheless, he considered that many degenerations belong to the active processes. Degenerations end up in 'indurations' (316-319). He also described 'necrosis', 'fatty metamorphosis' (a form of 'necrobiosis') and 'fatty degeneration'. In Lecture XVI, he expanded on 'fatty degeneration', 'cloudy swelling', 'atheromatous degeneration', 'pathological calcification' (or 'petrifaction'), and 'pathological ossification'. In Lecture XVII, Virchow introduced 'amyloid change' ('lardaceous' and 'waxy' degenerations) and dealt with inflammation. In Lecture XVIII, he introduced the 'Pathologic Reaction' of tubercle, and added the term hyperplasiae to refer to the formation of new cells. In Lecture XIX, he introduced the concepts of 'neoplasia' and 'retrograde metamorphosis'. Retrograde metamorphosis is not clearly defined and appears to corresponds to the evolution of the necrotic center of a tumor, tubercle, or pus. He also considered production of pus a Pathological Process. Finally, in Lecture XX, he discussed the terminology of new formations and introduced the term 'cheese metamorphosis'. It appears, then, that Virchow uttered the 'last word' on Pathological Processes at the middle of the nineteenth century. However, his conceptualizations were only slowly adopted in future years.

Throughout the rest of the nineteenth century, knowledge of the Pathological Processes at the cellular level evolved following the lines dictated by Virchow. But it was not until the first half of twentieth century that complete physiological and biochemical explanations were fully incorporated into their interpretation. Before WWII, the advances were evaluated by Sigerist in 1932. He addressed their pathogenesis, classified them, and used the term "Pathological Reactions." He considered that they are the result of pathological stimuli, different from a physiological one, and manifest at the cell and the organism level. At the cellular level, such reactions are regressive (degeneration and necrosis) and progressive (cell growth and multiplication). At the organ level, they are developmental/growth (malformations), functional (metabolic, circulatory disturbances, and disturbances of the nervous function), and defensive and healing processes (immunity/inflammation) (Sigerist 1932, 130-131). Following WWII, new technological developments made re-evaluation of the Processes necessary because until then the methodology to study cellular pathological changes relied on images obtained by light microscopy (Robbins and Cotran 1979, 1). Technological advances, such as the introduction of transmission electron microscopy, revolutionized the morphological descriptions of those images.

During these decades, the Pathological Processes evolved around the following groupings: Non-specific cell and tissue response to injury (inflammation, including tissue repair); Cellular adaptation (e.g., atrophy); Alteration of growth (e.g., hyperplasia/hypertrophy, neoplasia); Cellular death (e.g., necrosis/gangrene); Abnormal intracellular accumulation (e.g., calcification); Degeneration (e.g., cloudy swelling, fatty change, amyloid); Circulatory disturbance (e.g., edema, thrombosis, embolism); Cellular transformation (e.g., metaplasia); and Specific response to injury (e.g., hypersensitivity). A more recent classification of the Processes that deserves to be mentioned is: Cell injury and cell death, Inflammation and repair, Fluid and hemodynamic derangements, and Neoplasia (Robbins and Cotran 1979, ix).

Until 1980, the study of the Pathological Processes focused on the cellular membranes and the protoplasm, leaving the nucleus aside mainly because no technique could unravel its mystery. This was the state of knowledge up to the last quarter of the twentieth century before the introduction of molecular pathology. After 1980, the genetic material and its manifestations could be approached in the same manner as the membranes and protoplasm had been studied before.

Undoubtedly, molecular pathology techniques would eventually re-draw the history of the Pathological Processes as other technologies had done in the past. But how? The question is important, relevant, and makes sense when analyzing past events. All accepted concepts must be re-interpreted, no different from when the focus of attention was the 'tissue' around 1800 and the 'cell' in 1858. How would molecular testing and its knowledge product modify the conceptualization and identification of the Processes? Will mutations, deletions, etc., once their function is recognized, be enough to make a diagnosis? Will this technology make morphology, as we know now, irrelevant? Will the Processes disappear as specific entities? The answers to these questions will make the picture clear and of great didactic importance. The history presented here offers a baseline to understand why this could be so in the future. The answers rest on the shoulders of historians, years from now.

Examples of the historical beginnings of two Pathological Processes follow in the next two chapters. I have selected these examples from categories of their classification at the cellular level (Robbins and Cotran 1979, ix). The chosen examples are: Inflammation and Neoplasia.

CHAPTER 13

INFLAMMATION: ITS BEGINNIGS

Inflammation is a general cell and tissue response to injury because it is directed in the same manner to any kind of agent. It is a common pathway to the other Pathological Processes. Initially considered a disease, inflammation is the first Process recognized in history. In the first century of the C.E., Aulus Cornelius Celsus (ca 30 B.C.E.-38 C.E.), in *De re Medicina*, introduced the symptoms of rubor, tumor, calor, and dolor as indicative of inflammation. (Adami 1908, 375-376; Cappell 1964, 1; Cawson et al. 1989, 77). There is discussion about who introduced a fifth symptom, 'functio læsa' Some consider it was the Greek physician Titus Aufidius Siculus about 50 B.C.E. (Oertel 1927, 236); others mention Galen of Pergamon and Virchow (Robbins and Cotran 1979, 56; Cawson et al. 1989, 77; Chandrasoma and Taylor 1995, 35). These statements may give the impression that attention to the Process commenced at the beginnings of the C.E. This is not the case. Two thousand years before, pus, abscesses, and ulcers were described in the Egyptian's Edwin Smith Papyrus writings (ca. 550 B.C.E.). Hippocrates also made observations of inflammation and explained it with the humoral theory (Florey 1970,

22-24; Anderson 1971, 14-15). It was much later, in the seventeenth century, that the Dutch physician Boerhaave initiated a different explanation that is more in keeping with modern trends.

Herman Boerhaave's (1668-1738) interpretation followed Harvey's demonstration of the blood circulation. He considered that inflammation resulted from an obstruction of the blood vessels due to an increase in blood viscosity and to an increase in the force of the circulation. When unable to account for its effects, he brought back the humoral theory as explanation (Oertel 1927, 236-239). With the decline of this theory and its replacement with theoretical systems, Stahl, Hoffman, and Cullen offered explanations based on the actions of the nervous and vascular systems. Up to that date, inflammation was considered a disease, a conceptualization that was transformed by John Hunter. He changed this conceptualization into that of a Pathological Process and experimentally demonstrated the role of the blood vessels (Mackintosh 1844, 15-18). Both contributions were reinforced by the Paris School of medicine, while the Vienna School called attention to the role of cells in exudates. Virchow firmly established the latter role later (Oertel 1927, 236-239).

Following Virchow, Cohnheim and Metchnikoff made crucial contributions on explaining the mechanism of inflammation. Cohnheim, who published his findings on *Lectures on General Pathology* in 1877, experimentally determined the role of the blood vessels and the emigration of cells through the vascular wall (Florey 1970, 22-24). Though René Joachim Henry Dutrochet (1776-1847) in

1824 and Augustus Volney Waller (1816-1870) in 1842 had already described these findings, they did not do it as systematically as Cohnheim (Wagner 1876, 248-249; Coats 1883, 89; Ziegler 1883, 141; Stengel 1900, 101-102). But it was Metchnikoff who definitely demonstrated the participation of cells as found in the lectures he delivered at the Pasteur Institute in 1892. Metchnikoff considered inflammation a Pathological Process. The main theme presented was "the history of the evolution of inflammation" as a biological theory supported by Darwin's ideas (Metchnikoff 1968).

Other relevant findings that have impacted the history of inflammation are the participation of microorganisms, typification of specialized cells, and granuloma formation. The role of microorganisms is due to Pasteur's studies on fermentation and putrefaction and their identification in the second half of the nineteenth century (Dible 1950, 4-6). An example of specialized cells is the Langhans' cell, first described by Theodor Langhans (1839-1915) when experimenting with blood extravasation in animals. The term 'granuloma' was introduced by Virchow (Ziegler 1883, 163). A related term, 'tubercle', first mentioned by M. Baillie in London and Bayle in Paris, was applied to lesions of pulmonary tuberculosis (Oertel 1927, 273).

By 1880, three theories that would explain inflammation were in vogue (Metchnikoff 1968, viii). Virchow's 'nutritional theory' proposed that inflammation resulted from disturbed nutritional alterations of parenchymal cells and their proliferative response. The inflammatory cells were of this origin and the formation of a 'tumor', one of the manifestations of inflammation, would be thus explained. Metchnikoff's 'biological theory' assumed that phagocytosis would explain not only the beginnings of inflammation but also the subsequent reaction. In contrast, Cohnheim's 'vascular theory' supported that the immediate reason for inflammation to occur was an initial damage to the vascular wall. (Metchnikoff 1968, 6, 180-189). These were the historical conditions up to the last part of the nineteenth century.

The eventual understanding of the etiopathogenesis of inflammation began with the experimental studies of Cohnheim in the second half of the nineteenth century who described the Process as occurring in three phases: vascular, cellular, and tissular. The description formed the basis for further experimentation and interpretation in the twentieth century, becoming more detailed and sophisticated in relation to the role of the blood cells, the plasma, the vascular wall, and the tissues. Healing was incorporated to inflammation and also properly evaluated. Humoral factors were described and added to the explanation. These advances were only possible when contributory sciences and new technology were applied to animal experiments and the findings extrapolated to humans.

CHAPTER 14

NEOPLASIA: ITS BEGINNINGS

Neoplasms have been recognized since antiquity. They are reported in the papyri of Smith (1600 B.C.E.) and Eberts (1500 B.C.E.); in the Indian, Persian, Babylonian, and Greek literature; in Herodotus's The Histories (c 430 B.C.E.); and by embalmers in Egyptian mummies (Ewing 1940, 1-8; Mukherjee 2011). Breast cancer was one of the most common reported cases. Using the humoral theory of disease, Galen proposed that cancer originated in a deposit of black bile. This proposal was popular while this author dominated medical thought; that is, from the beginnings of the Common Era to the Renaissance (Mukherjee 2011, 47-48). During that time, surgical techniques and local chemical treatments had also advanced (Ewing 1940, 1-8). Galen's theory was challenged, among others, by the iatro-chemists (Paracelsus) and authors of the theoretical (rationalistic) systems of disease like Stahl, Hoffmann, Cullen and Brown. However, it was the idea that cancer originated in coagulated lymph that finally replaced black bile as the dominant belief. This idea intertwined with the concepts of 'vitalism' and 'spontaneous generation' and was supported by W. Hunter and the members of the Paris School. It was postulated that, locally, the lymph becomes hard or 'scirrhus', and it is this hardening that transform into cancer (Handley 1931, 1-2). The Paris School contributed with other theories; for instance, by attributing the cause to inflammation (Broussais), a secretion (Andral), a malignant degeneration (Cruveilhier), transformation of fibrin (Andral), and many others. Bichat also participated by distinguishing between tumor's parenchyma and stroma. It is during this scenario that the Germans began their experimental research on the existence of the cell as the unit of biological organization, moving the explanation of neoplasia to the third stage of positivism (Ewing 1940, 1-8; Chandrasoma and Taylor 1995, 256).

When Virchow introduced cellular pathology at the middle of the nineteenth century, coagulated lymph was left behind. Before him, tumor morphology was described only by gross features. By focusing on the cell and using the microscope systematically, he expanded the field of morphology by incorporating histology to the description. The approach revolutionized the field, having an effect on the terminology, causality, pathogenesis, and classification of neoplasia.

The influence of cellular pathology on 'terminology' can be divided into two eras, before and after Virchow. Before him, the term 'tumor' referred to inflammatory collections, tubercles, cysts, neoplasms, etc. (Gross 1857, 148; Ziegler 1883, 196; Krumbhaar [1937] 1962). In the case of 'neoplasms', particular terms were designated according to their gross appearance, such as carcinomas and sarcomas. The term 'carcinoma' (karkinos) was introduced by Hippocrates in reference to the peripheral infiltration of a superficial tumor manifested by dilated subcutaneous veins that, accordingly, simulated the legs of a crab (Mukherjee 2011, 47-48). The term 'sarcoma' referred to the tumor's similarity to flesh, that is, muscle and fat (Councilman, 143-144). After Virchow, new terms appeared as a result of the influence of cellular pathology and the use of the microscope. Terms like "anaplasia" was introduced by David Paul von Hansemann (1858-1920) in 1893 (Boyd 1970, 249), and "carcinoma in situ" by Albert Compton Broders (1885-1964) in 1932 (Broders 1932, 1670-1674; Wright Jr. 2012, 1437-1446).

Since the eighteenth century, external 'causes' of neoplasia of a varied nature have been reported, such as chronic irritation, chemicals, parasites, viruses, and radiation. Virchow systematized the idea that tumors arose from a non-specific chronic irritation. In his 'irritation theory', he proposed that this agent eventually made neighboring tissues lose control of the irritated area which would transform from reparation and regeneration into a neoplasm (Wright 1958, 495). The first reported specific agent was of a chemical nature. In London in 1775, Percival Pott (1714-1788) noted an increased incidence of scrotal cancer in chimney workers, suggesting that the chronic contact with tar was responsible. In Japan in 1917, the role of tar was established by Katsusaburo Yamagiwa (1863-1930) and Kōichi Ichikawa (1888-1948); they painted the ear of a rabbit with tar for several months until it produced the disease (Oertel 1927, 401; Cappell 1964, 145-146; Anderson 1971, 556). Fourteen years later, in 1931, Kennaway, Cook, and Hieger extracted the carcinogen responsible for the lesion, benzpyrene (a polycyclic aromatic hydrocarbon) (Cappell 1964, 146; Boyd 1970, 123-124; Robbins and Cotran 1979, 172-173). Another reported agent, now only of historical importance, is a parasite. In 1913, Johannes Andreas Grib Fibiger (1867-1928) produced squamous cell carcinoma in rats' stomachs by giving them cockroaches infested with a nematode worm. This experience, although not reproduced by other researchers, won him the Nobel Prize in 1926 (Handley 1931, 75; Boyd 1938, 286). Viruses were added to the list of causal agents. The demonstration of the viral participation began with animal experimentation. In 1911, Francis Peyton Rous (1879-1970) demonstrated that a neoplasm in fowls could be transferred with a cell-free filtrate (Rous 1911, 397-411). This was accepted as evidence of the presence of a viral particle in the filtrate. Other experimenters confirmed such transmission in birds, frogs, and other animals. In 1932, Richard Edwin Shope (1901-1966) demonstrated that a cutaneous papilloma in rabbits was transmitted by a virus (Shope 1932, 793-802). The same was done by John Joseph Bittner (1904-1961) who demonstrated the viral transmission of a mammary cancer in mice through breastfeeding (Bittner 1942, 462-463). Eventually, viral causality was demonstrated in humans, like the Epstein-Barr virus causing Burkitt's lymphoma and nasopharyngeal carcinoma (Ritchie 1990, 290, Mukherjee 2011, 174-175). Lastly, radiation as a carcinogen had become evident since the introduction of X-rays. The first malignancy was reported in 1907, twelve years after the discovery of X-rays in 1895 (Handley 1931, 145). The effect of radiation was again revealed with the exposure, between 1930 and 1950, to intravenous injection of a radio-opaque material (thorotrast) that caused hepatic hemangiosarcomas twenty years later (Wright 1958, 511; McManus 1966, 88-89). In the same category, lung cancer developed by exposure to radium in the mineworkers of Saxony and Bohemia and by the ingestion of this element and mesothorium by clock painters (McManus 1966, 185).

Tumorogenesis and tumor's 'classification' were also influenced by cellular pathology. Responsibility for 'oncogenesis' had swung between immune surveillance and the cell itself. The role of immune surveillance was put forward by Paul Ehrlich in 1909 and cell transformation - initially as a progressive two-stage process - by Rous and Kidd in 1941. Both mechanisms were refined with time, and became complementary (King 1983, 302, 318). Tumor 'classification' has a history by itself. It was common for each author of a pathology textbook to propose a classification of his own. But conceptually, only three are representative of the historical evolution of this issue. The first was introduced by Virchow who divided tumors into three categories according to if they arose from a single tissue, an organ, or monstruosities: histoid, organoid, and teratoid respectively (Councilman 1912,144). The second, proposed by Oertel, was according to the embryological layer from which the tumor supposedly arose. The third was based on the assumed cell/tissue of origin; that is, histogenesis.

Following these developments, the molecular understanding of neoplastic cell transformation expanded. An explosion of experimental and clinical information would mount on these developments in the years to follow.

When morphology was the only tool of investigation, the old question of the nature of cancer, whether a problem of differentiation or growth, was not resolved until the contribution of molecular pathology.

CHAPTER 15

PATHOLOGIC KNOWLEDGE IS SCIENTIFIC KNOWLEDGE

Pathologic knowledge can be evaluated using "judgments in terms of external criteria" that consist of the "evaluation of material with reference to selected or remembered criteria. ... or the comparison of the work with other works in the field" (Bloom et al. 1956, 190). I have accomplished the evaluation by comparing four scientific concepts introduced by Kuhn in *The Structure of Scientific Revolutions* (Kuhn 1996) with four selected conceptualizations of the pathologic knowledge. I consider that if such conceptualizations are similar, I would regard pathologic knowledge equivalent to, but independent of, scientific knowledge. By regard I understand the reasonable conclusion that, in spite of their differences, the concepts are qualitatively identical.

In his 1962 publication, Thomas Samuel Kuhn (1922-1996) presented a widely debated model about the progression of scientific knowledge. His work became the reference against which other models of progression were tested in the second half of the twentieth century. Among them, they were Lakatos's 'research programme' and Laudan's 'problem solving' (Laudan 1977; Lakatos 1985; Kuhn 1996; Fuller 2006). Kuhn's *Structure* changed the historical direction of scientific knowledge research, a topic that today is at the forefront of the history literature. The model created conceptualizations based on this kind of knowledge that are still popular despite the length of time after his publication.

15.1 *Kuhn's model of progression of knowledge*

In *The Structure*, Kuhn envisaged the progression of scientific knowledge as a series of 'revolutions', continuing ideas originally introduced in 1935 by Ludwik Fleck (1896-1961) (Fleck [1935] 1981; Kuhn 1996, viii-ix). I chose four of Kuhn's concepts, searching for their similarities and dissimilarities in pathologic knowledge. The concepts chosen were normal science, scientific facts, paradigms, and revolutions (Klee 1997, 129-155). 'By 'normal science' he meant, "... research firmly based upon one or more past scientific achievements, achievements that some particular scientific community acknowledges for a time as supplying the foundation for its further practice. ..." (Kuhn 1996, 10). Fleck had previously described normal science, although he did not use that name (Fleck [1935] 1981, 27-38). According to Kuhn, this is the kind of information found in textbooks, but are not useful for studying the evolution of scientific knowledge. He considered 'scientific facts' - the source of knowledge - to be socially constructed. 'Paradigm' or to use Fleck's term "scientific fact," is one of the most popular and controversial concepts of his proposals (Fleck [1935] 1981, xxviii, 84-98; Kuhn 1996, 23-34). Unfortunately, he provides several definitions that become difficult to apply, with paradigms at times described as theories and at other times as beliefs and values (Hacking 1985, 2; Kuhn 1996, 10; Okasha 2002, 81; Fuller 2006, 194). One definition of a paradigm is, "… universally recognized scientific achievements that for a time provide model problems and solutions to a community of practitioners. …" (Kuhn 1996, x). Finally, 'scientific revolutions' are "… those non-cumulative developmental episodes in which an older paradigm is replaced in whole or in part by an incompatible new one" (92). When paradigms start to be questioned, scientific revolutions begin (43-51). Transition to a new paradigm is not an accumulative process that transforms the old paradigm but a new framework to investigate the same data as before. Emergence of a new paradigm is no different from emergence of a discovery and may occur in short or long periods of time (77-91). Revolutions are not spontaneous events. They involve processes in which a scientific community practicing 'normal science' is confronted with anomalies or a crisis that makes it change its attitude toward the current paradigm and enter a phase of extraordinary research. The end result of a revolution is a new paradigm.

15.2 *Interpretation of the comparison*

Kuhn's examples were not biological; they came from the physical sciences including physics and astronomy. Yet, his definition of 'normal science' is applied to pathologic knowledge. A "… research firmly based upon one or more past scientific achievements" could correspond to the knowledge developed after the introduction of the 'cell theory' in AP by Virchow. Kuhn denied that the history of that research could be obtained from textbooks because they are useless as a source of primary data (Kuhn 1996, xi). To be fair, he appeared to modify his opinion years later (Fleck [1935] 1979, ix). As discussed in the Introduction, this information, contrary to Kuhn's opinion, is a source of data for uncovering the historical progression of pathologic knowledge. Such descriptions illustrate the important advances offered by experts at particular times, leaving aside knowledge that does not have continuity and becomes historically irrelevant. It demonstrates that pathologic knowledge did not grow by simple accumulation; rather it has been modified throughout history. This is clearly evident in the history of neoplasia in which the initial explanations given were continually modified and confirmed only when the development and application of new technology became more sophisticated and focused on the cell. I contend, therefore, that what is found in a textbook is the history of the emergence, development, consolidation, and maturity of pathologic knowledge.

Different from Kuhn, in our understanding of pathologic knowledge a 'scientific fact' is an abstraction obtained from an experimental experience that is reproducible and accepted by the scientific world (King 1982, 257-259). It is the combination of empiricism and rationalism and their interpretation depends on the accepted opinion in a particular era. Facts are objective and have existed, for instance, in the third century B.C.E. and in the twentieth century. It is their interpretation that has evolved over time. New technology progressively improved their investigation, detection, and characteristics, even at micro levels of observation. This is illustrated with the introduction of light and electron microscopy at different periods. Not observed by the naked eye, a blue color stain by H&E in a cell under the light microscope detected the same fact by the end of the nineteenth century than in the second half of the twentieth when the electron microscopy demonstrated that the blue color corresponds to abundant rough endoplasmic reticulum. Although the facts are the same, they manifest differently according to the technology involved in their detection and, as a consequence, the interpretation differs. Refinement of the facts occurred multiple times in history. It is this refinement that we accept as 'accumulation'. It also denies the process of "simple" accumulation, which Kuhn ascribes to data obtained from textbooks. Instead, it demonstrates a qualified accretion, which is the gradual linear accumulation of particular knowledge identified *a posteriori*. This accretion is described in the evolution of the understanding of inflammation. The gradual accumulation of knowledge about the role of the vascular wall, blood flow, and cells has the following qualifications: it is selective, since only certain knowledge is accumulated;

it is progressive, because the accumulation develops step by step; and it evolves, from simple to complex, from less to more elaborate, from good to better, from macro to micro. Facts are confirmed and re-confirmed by experimentation. The progress of attaining knowledge is infinite, and constantly changing (Fleck 1979, 64). It is a naturalistic view in which the only reality is organized matter.

The closest example of Kuhn's paradigm, "recognized scientific achievements that for a time provide model problems and solutions," is Virchow's 'cellular theory'. It has remained valid since the middle of the nineteenth century. But, is Virchow's 'cellular theory' a paradigm or not? It certainly created a revolution in the literal sense of the word but not according to Kuhn's understanding that revolutions are non-cumulative events. Cell theory was compatible with the 'organ' and 'tissue' theory that preceded it. No different than in Morgagni's *Seats and Causes of Disease*, its history was a cumulative event. In his *Lectures*, Virchow claimed to be building on knowledge accumulated since the middle of the eighteenth century (Virchow [1858] 1978, xiv). And certainly, this was the case. Since the 1830s, for instance, the cell had replaced the fiber as the biological unit, the light microscope began to be introduced systematically, and it was accepted that a cell evolved from another cell (McMenemey 1968, 16-34).

Perhaps the introduction of scientific/technological developments such as 'light microscopy', 'bacteriology', 'electron microscopy', and 'immunobiology' (i.e., contributory biomedical knowledge) would be identified as paradigms. Certainly, they have promoted re-evaluation of accepted facts and expanded and rectified previous knowledge. However, these advances were developed independently of AP and, when introduced into this science, replaced nothing, nor were they the result of anomalies. On the contrary, all were applied simultaneously as soon as they were available and became incorporated. They appear closer to innovations within a prevalent opinion, as we accept in this compendium, rather than paradigms. In addition, pathologists do not debate if the cell theory is correct or not, but use it to expand knowledge of disease, and this is contrary to Kuhn's opinion that a paradigm is continuously evaluated during the period of normal science.

The argument that knowledge did not progress by 'revolutions' was contemporaneous with Kuhn's thesis. A historiographic model called the "gradualist" considers that, historically, knowledge accumulates slowly and selectively, and is maintained in a reservoir that contributes to refining what is considered truth at one particular time (Laudan 1977, 139). Our review is closer to this conceptualization as illustrated with the history of inflammation. In the second half of the eighteenth century, Hunter radically changed the concept of disease into a Pathological Process. A century later, Cohnheim designed an experiment whose conclusions became the gold standard to study it. Almost a century later, electron microscopy and biochemistry, using Cohnheim's model, clarified the intimate mechanism of the Process. This history corresponds to Laudan's gradualist proposal.

Another example that tends to refute the idea that pathologic knowledge progresses by revolutions can be found in Virchow's account of his own experience published in *Cellular Pathology*. In Lecture X, he describes Cruveilhier's explanation of leucocytes moving from the center to the periphery of blood vessels by capillary attraction. Cruveilhier's partial explanation is full of conjectures to fill the gaps in his doctrine of phlebitis, namely, that the primary lesion rested on the vascular wall. Virchow used his experimental results to explain such gaps, and proposed his own theory based on new facts derived from experiment (Virchow [1860] 1978, 197-198). He only modified Cruveilhier's explanation, and the new interpretation was accepted and has persisted. In Lecture XV, Virchow also illustrates how science evolves when improved technology (i.e., microscopy) corrects previous statements; and how his cellular theory corrects the prevalent theory of stasis, i.e., confusing degenerated renal tubular cells with a blood vessel containing stagnating content (Virchow [1860] 1978, 338-339). Our interpretation agrees with those of Virchow. Progression was not obtained by revolutions.

15.3 *Conclusion*

The evaluation indicates that four of Kuhn's conceptualizations of the progression of scientific knowledge here considered (i.e., normal science, scientific facts, paradigms, and revolutions) show similarities and dissimilarities with those uncovered in the history of the foundational knowledge in AP. This knowledge is found in textbooks and is the one that introduces a neophyte into the specialty during a period of training. 'Normal science' as found in textbooks is a valid source of historical data. The 'cell theory' is the closest event similar to a 'paradigm', although its appearance does not display characteristics of a 'revolution'. The production of 'scientific facts' in AP is an empiricist-rationalist approach that relies on observation and experimentation. The history of these facts qualifies for describing the progression of pathologic knowledge as found in textbooks. Such history does not progress by revolutions, but by a selective, progressive, and evolving accretion of knowledge identified *a posteriori*. Nevertheless, in spite of the dissimilarities of Kuhn' concepts with those in pathologic knowledge, the similarities overcome the dissimilarities, making it reasonable to conclude that pathological knowledge can be recognized as independent scientific knowledge.

EPILOGUE

This compendium is a document about "What is AP" built from the historical evidence on pathologic knowledge and its context (biographies and institutions). The evidence is organized around the 'biomedical' model of disease, the model used by pathologists when practicing basic and clinical sciences and the one taught in training. It unravels how pathologists think, what they do, and what AP "is" for them.

The compendium is not a textbook. It deals with the British-North American history of the foundational knowledge of the specialty since its beginnings in the 1500s. The history describes how pathologic knowledge evolved to be a division of scientific knowledge. Consequently, AP can be considered a system of scientific knowledge because pathologic knowledge is used to draw conclusions about certain manifestations of disease (Duffin 2010, 65). The consideration is complementary to the definition of pathology introduced by Malkin and discussed in Chapter 3 (Malkin 1993, 8).

Anatomic aspects that would correspond to AP were noticeable since the Middle Ages, acquiring impetus at the Renaissance. It took two and a half centuries, from the sixteenth to the middle of the eighteenth, for this knowledge to evolve into what eventually became known as AP. Up to the eighteenth century, Italians contributed the most to its development. That being said, AP can be traced to Morgagni, followed by the German Virchow who introduced 'cellular pathology' as modern AP in the middle of the nineteenth century. Among the English-speaking countries, the major contributions in the twentieth century were by the Americans, after an initial impetus by the Germans.

AP, as a branch of anatomy, has maintained its identity as a morphological science since its beginnings in the 1500s. Nevertheless, its identity was challenged by scientific/technological

innovations (i.e., contributory biomedical knowledge and techniques) such as physiology, bacteriology, immunobiology, radiology, electron microscopy, etc. The influence was so great that to the title "department of pathology" was added "and bacteriology," "and immunobiology." As a result of advances in electron microscopy in the 1970s, there was the suggestion to create a new pathology called "organelle pathology." When new radiological procedures such as "Computer Tomography Scan" (CTS) and "Magnetic Resonance Imaging" (MRI), began to appear, I heard that AP will become useless because diagnosis in vivo will be enough. The challenges have been unsuccessful. Today, the influence of genetics has made it possible to add the term "and molecular pathology" to the title of departments. But, will genetics change the identity of AP as a morphological science?

Opinions are diverse among anatomic pathologists, from those who think that AP will be transformed into a branch of genetics to those who deny that possibility; however, both groups cannot explain how it will happen. Given the diverse opinions, the issue of genetics seems as transcendental as the influence of previous scientific/technological developments. This issue cannot be disregarded because it has implications; such as for the classification of AP within the sciences, on administrative considerations that may impact its professional position in the health care system, in modification of curricula for training pathologists and other health care professionals, for terminology, and so forth.

The history in the compendium ends when molecular pathology techniques to study the genome began to make an impact. Before, the morphological study of organ/tissue/cell was based on phenotype. Direct analysis of the genome and its manifestations was not a familiar idea, although morphological techniques were used to study the nucleus. By using light microscopy, mitosis, karyorrhexis, karyolysis, and multinucleation were recognized. By electron microscopy, these appearances and the distinction between eu- and hetero-chromatin were confirmed. Another morphological technique designed to study the chromosomes was karyotyping, although usually not performed by anatomic pathologists. It was in the 1970s that techniques to study the molecular composition of the genome began to be developed (*in situ* Hybridization), then followed by the Southern Blot (Pardue and Gall 1970, 1356-1358; Southern 1975, 503-517). In the 1980s, this technology exploded with the introduction of gene cloning techniques through which fragments of DNA can be copied in large quantities. The Polymerase Chain Reaction (PCR), developed in its current form by Kary Banks Mullis (1944-2019), is the best known of these techniques (Divan and Royds 2016, 22, 26, 28). Given the time frame the compendium covers, it sets the historical basis on which the discussion about the role of genetics on the specialty can be obtained.

I consider that to reach a reasonable conclusion, arguments must be organized around the experience offered by 'history' and by a systematic 'analysis' of the issue. Historically, it is demonstrated that the challenges presented by physiology, bacteriology, immunobiology, and electron microscopy, eventually disappeared because they were incorporated into pathology and the specialty did not lose its morphological identity. On the other hand, given its relevance, oncologists and non-oncologists may argue that the future of tumor diagnosis rests on using only a mutation, a translocation, clonality, and so on. A counter argument comes to my mind. I personally think that even if they are correct, there will still be room for an important morphological contribution. Neoplastic diseases are only one class among several other classes of diseases (e.g., infectious, metabolic, immunological, traumatic [forensic pathology], psychiatric, etc.). The other classes will persist with the participation of AP because it is Nature that decides. This is the experience with infectious diseases. History teaches us that when sulphas and antibiotics came into practice in the 1930's, cardiovascular and neoplastic diseases replaced infectious diseases. Bacteriology, as science, did not disappear; it only evolved into today's Infectious Diseases. Therefore, when controlled, neoplastic diseases will be replaced by other classes. This is the lesson of history.

Analytically, the controversy, in my opinion, is due to a partial analysis of reality. For a total analysis, it is necessary to include four perspectives: AP as 'science', AP as 'practice' (e.g., surgical and cytopathology), 'genetics' *per se*, and 'molecular pathology'. Although a focused view of the subject, it is necessary to include these perspectives to facilitate the analysis that also is applicable to sub-specialties of AP. The interaction of the four perspectives not only adds to clarify the controversy but also to come to a reasonable conclusion. As a 'science', AP will be influenced greatly by 'genetics'. Its application corresponds to the study of genes and their consequences using molecular pathology techniques. Pathologic knowledge will be enriched. Concepts will be re-evaluated. Translational research will be applied more frequently. As 'practice', the influence of genetics will correspond to the use of molecular diagnostic methods. The technical advances of 'molecular pathology' will only improve its importance in diagnosis. Its contributions to personalized medicine will be enhanced. New classifications of diseases will be created. In conclusion, the analysis does not support the argument that AP will lose its morphological identity.

It is too early to write the history of the full impact of genetics on AP as a field of science and practice, although literature is already published on this medical topic (Vollmer and Goldmann 2011, 223-230; Mukherjee 2011; 2016). With the contribution of genetics, AP - as science - will continue maturing. As in the past, the scientific/technological contributions of other fields did the same without destroying the morphological essence of the specialty. AP - as practice - will rely on molecular diagnostic methods that will become ancillary as embodied in the current title of the International Society for IHC and Molecular Morphology and its

Journal. Its mission statement says, "The Society will promote knowledge, innovation and excellence in slide-based techniques such as immunohistochemistry and in situ hybridization. ..." (ISIHCMM n.d.). The practice of surgical and cytopathology will evolve with the incorporation of molecular morphology, the addition of better-quality assurance programs, the participation in personalized medicine, by improvements on anatomoclinical correlation using standardized protocols, and advances in telepathology, Artificial Intelligence, etc.

Based on this historical and analytical evidence, experience makes me conclude that genetics, through the scientific developments obtained by molecular pathology techniques, will influence AP no differently than previous scientific/technological advances and, therefore, its morphological essence as science and as practice will prevail. Enthusiasm should not distance us from the term "anatomical' that continues being an accurate term. After all, Virchow's "cellular pathology," the current quasi-paradigm, includes the nucleus and its content.

GLOSSARY

*CONCEPTUALIZATION: The linguistic expression of a system of ideas.

*DETERMINE: A 'verb' that refers to the cause of a phenomenon that controls its occurrence in a certain manner.

*EMPIRICISM: A term that refers to experience as the only source of knowledge.

*EMPIRICISM/RATIONALISM: The accept source of knowledge.

*ESSENCE: The knowledge that tells us what AP is.

*EXPERIENCE: Knowledge and skill obtained in practice.

*EXPLANATORY REDUCTIONISM: The explanation that the morphology of the body's compartments (i.e., organ, tissue, cell) facilitates the assessment of structure and function in an integrated manner.

*HUMOURALISM: Also known as "humourism", is an explanation that considers disease the result of an unbalance of four humours presents in the body. The humors are blood, yellow bile, black bile, and phlegm (mucus). This doctrine, introduced by Galen, persisted more than 1300 years and continued in a revised form in the sixteenth century and in a declined form in the seventeenth, although remnants were still found in the eighteenth and the first half of the nineteenth centuries.

*MATTERS OF FACT: Are objective and verifiable observations. They are the empirical basis on which perception is based and reasoning is founded.

*MECHANISM: A idea that considered human beings like machines.

*MENTAL REPRESENTATION: Knowledge stored in long-term memory in the form of discourses and images.

*MENTALITIES: The end-result of the production of knowledge and the one shared by a scientific community. Mentalities are based on empirical findings, but also on the interaction of perception, experience, and the climate of opinion in which a scientific group has developed.

*NATURE OF DISEASE: Understood as the structural and functional changes produced in the body by a disease and its manifestation as signs and symptoms.

*OBSERVATION: Is the process of collecting information by the process of perception using the senses with or without the aid of technology.

*PERCEPTION: Is the handling and interpretation of matter of facts using deduction, induction, and analogy, that is, reasoning. It refers only to sensory perceptions, with or without the aid of technology.

*POSITIVISM: A philosophical theory that considers that valid knowledge is obtained by observation and experimentation; that is, by the scientific method. Comte's positivism declares that human knowledge has evolved in three phases: theological, metaphysical, and positive.

*PROBLEM-SOLVING: An approach to a situation that demands a solution.

*RATIONALISM: A term that refers to the mind as the only source of knowledge.

REALISM: The school of thought that accepts that Nature is independent of our mind.

*REASONING: Is here considered the mental strategies utilized to approach the solution of a problem and is considered synonymous with 'mode of thinking' and 'thought process'.

*SCIENTIFIC KNOWLEDGE: The end product generated by the scientific method.

*SCIENTIFIC METHOD: An approach to obtain knowledge through observation and experimentation.

*SOLIDISM: The concept that 'the site and cause' of clinical manifestations of disease is the body's organs.

*SYSTEM OF KNOWLEDGE: An understanding of AP that consists of three elements: A 'system' (the procedures to obtain it, the scientific method); 'validated' by current science (the 'corpus' of knowledge) and by a philosophy (a 'climate of opinion', the context).

*TRUTH: In AP, a temporal belief that will be modified according to the role played by new hypotheses, new technology, and other ways of knowing.

*VITALISM: The postulation that an unknown force (a vital force, the soul) is responsible for maintaining life and health; that is, for the normal functioning of the body's organs.

REFERENCES

*Ackerknecht Erwin H. 1967. *Medicine at the Paris Hospital: 1794-1848*. Baltimore: The Johns Hopkins Press.

*------. 1982. *A Short History of Medicine*. Baltimore: The Johns Hopkins University Press.

*Adami, J. George. 1908. *The Principles of Pathology*, vol. 1. Philadelphia: Lea & Febiger.

*Agassi, Joseph. 1976. "Causality and Medicine." *Journal of Medical Philosophy*. 1 (4): 301- 317.

*Anderson, W.A.D., ed. 1971. *Pathology*, vol.1. 6th ed. St. Louis (MO): C.V. Mosby.

*Baillie, Matthew. (1812) n.d. *The Morbid Anatomy of Some of the Most Important Parts of the Human Body*. 4rd ed. London: W. Bulmer and Co. Reprint, United States: Kessinger Publishing's Legacy Reprints.

*------. (1803) n.d. *A Series of Engravings, Accompanied with Explanations, Which Are Intended to Illustrate the Morbid Anatomy of Some of the Most Important Parts of the Human Body; Divided into Ten Fasciculi*. London: W. Bulmer. Reprint, La Verge, Tennessee: Gale ECCO Print Editions.

*Bates, Don. 2009. "Medicine and the Soul of Science." *Canadian Bulletin of Medical History*. 26 (1): 23-84.

*Beaumont, William. (1833) 1959. *Experiments and Observations on the Gastric Juice and the Physiology of Digestion*. With a bibliographical essay by Sir William Osler. Reprint, New York: Dover Pub.

*Benivieni, Antonio. (1507) 1954. *De Abditis Nonnullis Ac Mirandis Morborum et Sanationum Causis*. Translated by Charles Singer with biographical appreciation by Esmond R Long. Springfield, Ilinois: Charles C. Thomas.

*Bernard, Claude. (1865) 1957. *An Introduction to the Study of Experimental Medicine*. Translated by H.C. Greene, with an introduction by L.J. Henderson and a foreword by I.B. Cohen. Reprint, New York: Dover.

*Bertolini, Meli Domenico. 2015. "The Rise of Pathological Illustrations: Baillie, Bleuland, and Their Collections." *Bulletin of the History of Medicine*. 89 (2): 209-242.

*Bichat, Xavier. (1813) 1987. *A Treatise on the Membranes in General, and on Different Membranes in Particular*. Translated by John G. Coffin, with an historical notice of the life and writings of the author by M. Husson. Cambridge: Hilliard & Metcalf. Reprint, Birmingham, Alabama: The Classics of Medicine Library.

*------. (1824) 2010. *General Anatomy, Applied to Physiology and the Practice of Medicine*. Translated by C. Coffyn, revised and corrected by G. Calvert. Paris: n.p. Reprint, La Vergne, Tennessee: General Books.

*------. 1827. *Pathological Anatomy*. Translated by Joseph Togno, collected and transcribed by Pierre Auguste Beclard in 1805, with a short account of Bichat's life by F. G. Boisseau. Philadelphia: J. Grigg. La Vergne, Tennessee: General Books, 2009.

*Bignold, Leon P., Brain L.D. Coghlan, and H.P.A. Jersmann. 2008. "Virchow's "Cellular Pathology" 150 Years Later." *Seminars in Diagnostic Pathology*. 25: 140-146.

*Bittner, John J. 1942. "The Milk-Influence of Breast Tumors in Mice." *Science*. 95 (2470): 462-463.

*Bliquez, Lawrence J., and Alexander Kazhdan. 1984. "Four Testimonia to Human Dissection in Byzantine times." *Bulletin of the History of Medicine*. 58: 554-557.

*Bloom, Benjamin S., Max D. Engelhart, Edward J. Furst, Walker H. Hill, and David R. Krathwohl., eds. 1956. *Taxonomy of Educational Objectives: The Classification of Educational Goals. Handbook I: Cognitive Domain*. New York: Longman Inc.

*Bonah, Christian. 1998. "Pathological Anatomy versus Pathological Physiology: A Franco-German Dispute over a 'Province for Pathology'." In Cay-Rüdiger Prull in collaboration with John Woodward 1998, 31-53.

*Boyd, William. 1938. *A Text-Book of Pathology: An Introduction to Medicine*. 3rd ed. Philadelphia: Lea & Febiger.

*Broders, Albert C. 1932. "Carcinoma In Situ Contrasted with Benign Penetrating Epithelium. *Journal of the American Medical Association*. 99: 1670-1674.

*Brown, Harold I. 1987. *Observation & Objectivity*. New York: Oxford University Press.

*Browning, Robert. 1985. ""Texts and Documents": A Further Testimony to Human Dissection in the Byzantine World." *Bulletin of the History of Medicine*. 59 (4): 518-520.

*Bunge, Mario. N.d. *La Ciencia, su Método, y su Filosofía*. Medellin (Colombia): Editorial Logos.

*Canguilhem, Georges. 2008. *Knowledge of Life*. Edited by Paola Marrati and Todd Meyers and translated by Stefanos Geroulanos and Daniela Ginsburg. New York: Fordham University.

*Cappell, D. F. 1964. *Muir's Textbook of Pathology*. 8th ed. London, UK: Edward Arnold.

*Cardwell, Donald. 2001. *Wheels, Clocks, and Rockets: A History of Technology*. New York: W. W. Norton.

*Carlino, Andrea. 1999. *Books of the Body: Anatomical Ritual and Renaissance Learning*. Translated by John Tedeschi and Anne C. Tedeschi. Chicago: University of Chicago Press.

*Carswell, Robert. 1838. *Pathological Anatomy: Illustrations of the Elementary Forms of Disease*. London (England): Longman, Orme, Brown, Green, Logman. books.google.com

*Castiglioni, Arturo. *A History of Medicine*. 1941. Translated and edited by E. B. Krumbhaar. New York: Alfred A. Knopf.

*Cawson, Roderick A., Alexander W. McCracken, Peter B. Marcus, and Ghazi S. Zaatari. 1989. *Pathology: The Mechanisms of Disease*. 2nd ed. St. Louis (MO): C. V. Mosby.

*Chambers, Mortimer, Raymond Grew, David Herlihy, Theodore K. Rabb, and Isser Woloch. 1983. *The Western Experience*. 3rd ed. New York: Alfred A. Knopf.

*Chan, John K. C. 2014. "The Wonderful Colors of the Hematoxylin-Eosin Stain in Diagnostic Surgical Pathology." *International Journal of Surgical Pathology*. 22(1): 12-32.

*Chandrasoma, Parakama and Clive R. Taylor. 1995. *Concise Pathology*. 2nd ed. Norwalk (CT): Appleton & Lange.

*Clossy, Samuel. (1763) 1967. *Observations on Some of the Diseases of the Parts of the Human Body: Chiefly Taken *from the Dissections of Morbid Bodies*. London: G. Kearsly. In *Samuel Clossy, M.D. (1724-1786), The Existing Works*. 1967. With a biographical sketch by Morris H. Saffron. New York: Hafner Publishing Company.

*Coats, Joseph. 1883. *A Manual of Pathology*. Philadelphia: Henry C. Lea's Son & Co. books.google.com.

*Cohnheim, Julius. 1889. *Lectures on General Pathology: A Handbook for Practitioners and Students*, vol 1. Translated by Alexander B. McKee. London: The New Sydenham Society.

*Cohrs, Raydall J., Tyler Martin, Parviz Ghahramani, et al. 2015. "Translational Definition by the European Society for Translational Medicine." *New Horizons in Translational Medicine*. 2: 86-88. htttp://dx.doi.org/10.1016/j.nhtm.2014.12.002

*Collingwood, Robin George. 1994. *The Idea of History*. Edited and introduction by Jan Van Der Dussen. Oxford: Oxford University Press.

*Conn, H. J. 1953. *Biological Stains: A Handbook on the Nature and Uses of the Dyes Employed in the Biological Laboratory*. 6th ed. Published for the Biological Stain Commission. Baltimore: Williams & Wilkins.

*Coons A.H., Creech H.J., and Jones R.N. 1941. "Immunological Properties of Antibody Containing a Fluorescent Group." *Proceedings Society Biology and Medicine*. 47: 200-202.

*Councilman, William Thomas. 1912. *Pathology: A Manual for Teachers and Students*. Boston: W. M. Leonard.

*Craigie, David. 1851. *Elements of General and Pathological Anatomy: Presenting a View of the Present*

State of Knowledge in These Branches of Science. 2d. ed. Philadelphia: Lindsay and Blakiston. books.google.com.

*Croft, William J. 2006. *Under the Microscope: A Brief History of Microscopy*. Singapore: World Scientific Pub.

*Cruikshank, William. 1786. *The Anatomy of the Absorbing Vessels of the Human Body*. London: Printed by G. Nicol, Bookseller to His Majesty, in the Stand. books.google.com

*Cunningham, Andrew. 2010. *The Anatomist Anatomis'd: An Experimental Discipline in Enlightenment Europe*. Surrey (England): Ashgate Pub.

*Delafield, Francis and T. Mitchell Prudden. 1901. *A Handbook of Pathological Anatomy and Histology: With an Introductory Section on Post-Mortem Examinations and the Methods of Preserving and Examining Diseased Tissues*. 6th ed. New York: William Wood.

*DeLanda, Manuel. 2015. *Philosophical Chemistry: Genealogy of a Scientific Field*. London (England): Bloomsbury.

*Dible, J. Henry. 1950. *Dible and Davie's Pathology: An Introduction to Medicine and Surgery*. 3rd ed. London (England): J. & A. Churchill Ltd.

*Divan, Aysha and Janice A. Royds. 2016. *Molecular Biology: A Very Short Introduction*. Oxford: Oxford University Press.

*Duffin, Jacalyn. 1998. *To See with a Better Eye: A life of R.T.H. Laennec*. Princeton (NJ): Princeton University Press.

*------. 2010. *History of Medicine: A Scandalously Short Introduction*. 2d ed. Toronto: University of Toronto Press.

*Erlandson, R. A. 1987. "Application of Transmission Electron Microscopy to Human Tumor Diagnosis: An Historical Perspective." *Cancer Investigation*. 5: 487-505.

*Ewing, James, 1940. *Neoplastic Diseases: A Treatise on Tumors*. 4th ed. Philadelphia: W. B. Saunders.

*Finkbeiner, Walter E., Phillip C. Ursell, and Richard L. Davis. 2008. *Autopsy Pathology: A Manual and Atlas*. 2d ed. Philadelphia: Elsevier.

*Fleck, Ludwik. (1935) 1981. *Genesis and Development of a Scientific Fact*. Edited by Thaddeus J. Trenn and Robert Merton. Translated by Fred Bradley and Thaddeus J. Trenn. Foreword by Thomas S. Kuhn. Chicago: The University of Chicago Press.

*Florey, H., ed. 1970. *General Pathology*. 4th ed. London (England): Lloyd-Luke (Medical Books).

*Forrester, John M. 1994. "The Homoeomerous Parts and Their Replacement by Bichat's Tissues." *Medical History*. 38: 444-458.

*Foster, W. D. 1959. "The Early History of Clinical Pathology in Great Britain." *Medical History*. 3: 173-187.

*Foucault, Michel. 1994. *The Birth of the Clinic: An Archaeology of Medical Perception*. Translated by A. M. Sheridan Smith. New York: Vintage Books.

*Fuller, Steve. 2006. *Kuhn vs. Popper: The Struggle for the Soul of Science*. Cambridge (England): Icon Books.

*Gantner, George E., Roger A. Côté, and R.S. Backett, eds. 1979. *SNOMED*. Chicago: College of American Pathologists.

*Garrison, Fieldging H. 1929. *An Introduction to the History of Medicine with Medical Chronology, Suggestions* *for Study and Bibliographic Data.* 4d ed. Philadelphia: W.B. Saunders.

*Gladstone, G.P. and E. P. Abraham. 1970. "Acquired Immunity: The Serological Reactions of Bacteria." In Florey 1970, 1021-1046.

*Green, T. Henry. 1881. *An Introduction to Pathology and Morbid Anatomy*. 4th ed. American edition from the Fifth revised and enlarged English edition. Philadelphia: Henry C. Lea's Son.

*Gross, Samuel D. 1857. *Elements of Pathological Anatomy*. 3rd ed. Philadelphia: Blanchard and Lea. books. google.com.

*Hacking, Ian, ed. 1985. *Scientific Revolutions*. Oxford: Oxford University Press.

*Haller, Albert. 1756. *Pathological Observations, Chiefly from Dissections of Morbid Bodies*. London (England): D. Wilson and T. Durham. books.google.com.

*Hamilton, D. J. 1889. *A Text-Book of Pathology: Systematic & Practical*. London: Macmillan. books. google.com.

*Handley, W. Sampson. 1931. *The Genesis of Cancer*. London (England): Kegan Paul, Trench, Trubner & Co.

*Hannam, James. 2011. *The Genesis of Science: How the Christian Middle Ages Launched the Scientific Revolution*. Washington (DC): Regnery Pub.

*Harris, Henry. 2000. *The Birth of the Cell*. London (England): Yale University Press.

*Harvey, William. (1616) 1961. *Lectures On the Whole of Anatomy*. An annotated translation of *Prelectiones Anatomiae Universalis* by C. D. O'Malley, F. N. L. Poynter and K. F. Russell. Berkeley: University of California Press.

*------. (1628) 1963. "Movement of the Heart and Blood in Animals: An Anatomical Essay." In *William Harvey: The Circulation of the Blood and other Writings.* Translation by Kenneth J. Franklin. London (England): Everyman's Lib.

*Hess, Volker. 1998. "Disease as Parasite: The Discovery of Time for a Theory of Pathology." In Cay-Rüdiger Prull in collaboration with John Woodward 1998, 13-14.

*Hewson, William. 1774. *Experimental Inquires: Part the First. Containing an Inquiry into the Properties of the Blood, with Remarks on Some of its Morbid Appearances: and an Appendix, Relating to the Discovery of the Lymphatic System in Birds, Fish, and the Animals called Amphibious.* 2d ed. London: Printed for J. Johnson, No. 72, St. Paul's Church-Yard. books.google.com.

*Himsworth, Harold. 1970. *The Development and Organization of Scientific Knowledge.* London (England): Heinemann.

*Hollman, Arthur.1995. "The Paintings of Pathological Anatomy by Sir Robert Carswell (1793-1857)." *British Heart Journal.* 74: 566-570.

*Hooke, Robert. 1667. *Micrographia: Or Some Physiological Descriptions of Minute Bodies Made by Magnifying Glasses with Observations and Inquires Thereupon.* London (England): John Martin and James Allestry, printer to the Royal Society. books.google.com.

*Hope, James. 1834. *Principles and Illustrations of Morbid Anatomy: Adapted to the Elements of M. Andral and to the Cyclopædia of Practical Medicine.* London (England):

Printed for Whittaker & Co., Ave-Maria Lane. books. google.com.

*Horner, William E. 1829. *A Treatise on Pathological Anatomy*. Philadelphia: Carey, Lea & Carey. books. google.com.

*Howell, Joel D. 1995. *Technology in the Hospital: Transforming Patient Care in the Early Twentieth Century*. Baltimore: The John Hopkins University Press.

*Irons, Ernest E. 1942. "Theophile Bonet 1620-1689. His Influence on the Science and Practice of Medicine." *Bulletin of the History of Medicine*. 12 (5): 623-665.

*Jackson, S.H. 1792. *Dermato-pathologia*. London (England): H. Reynell, J. Robson and J. Johnson.

*ISIHCMM (International Society for IHC and Molecular Morphology). n.d. *Mission Statement and Bylaws*. N.p.: ISIHCMM. Accessed Dec 18, 2021, https:// isimm.org.

*Karamanou M, Liappas I, Stamboulis E, Lymperi M, Kyiakis K, and Androutros G. 2012. "Sir Robert Carswell (1793-1857): Coining the Term "Melanoma"." *Journal of Balkan Union on Oncology*. 17(2): 400-402.

*Keel, Othmar. 2001. *L'avenement de la médicine clinique moderne en Europe: 1750-1815*. Montreal: Les Presses de l'Université de Montréal.

*Kim, Jaegwon. 1995. "Explanation." In Audi, Robert. 1998. The Cambridge Dictionary of Philosophy, 256-257. Cambridge: Cambridge University Press.

*King, Lester S. 1971. *A History of Medicine: Selected Readings*. Middlesex (England): Penguin Books.

*------. 1982. *Medical Thinking: A Historical Preface*. Princeton (NJ): Princeton University Press.

*King, Lester S. and Marjorie C. Meehan. 1973. "A History of the Autopsy: A Review." *American Journal of Pathology*. 73 (2): 514-544.

*King, Donald West, Cecilia M. Fenoglio, and Jay H. Lefkowitch. 1983. *General Pathology: Principles and Dynamics*. Philadelphia: Lea & Febiger.

*Klee, Robert. 1997. *Introduction to the Philosophy of Science: Cutting Nature at its Seams*. New York: Oxford University Press.

*Klemke, E. D., Robert Hollinger, David Wÿss Rudge, and A. David Kline, eds. 1998. *Introductory Readings in the Philosophy of Science*. 3rd ed. Amherst (NY): Prometheus Books.

*Klemperer, Paul. 1958. ""The Fielding H. Garrison Lecture": The Pathology of Morgagni and Virchow." *Bulletin of the History of Medicine*. 32: 24-38.

*Krumbhaar, E. B. (1937) 1962. *Pathology*. Clio Medica, no. 19. N.p.: Paul B. Hoeber. Reprint, New York: Hafner Pub.

*Kuhn, Thomas S. 1996. *The Structure of Scientific Revolutions*. 3d ed. Chicago: The University of Chicago Press.

*Laennec, René-Théophile-Hyacinthe. 1884. *Traité inédit sur l'anatomie pathologique or exposition des altérations visibles qu'éprouve le corps humain dans l'état de maladie*. Introduction et premier chapitre précédés d'une préface par V. Compiled by Mèriadec Laënnec and Victor Cornil. Paris: Félix Alcan.

*Lain Entralgo, Pedro. 1978. *Historia de la medicina*. Barcelona: Masson and Salvat.

*Lakatos, Imre. 1985. "History of Science and its Rational Reconstructions." In Hacking 1985, 115-123.

*Laudan, Larry. 1977. *Progress and Its Problems: Towards a Theory of Scientific Growth*. Berkeley: University of California Press.

*Lawrence, Sherwook H. 1989. "The Early History of Soluble Factors." In Mazumdar 1989, 221-290.

*Lawrence, Susan C. 1996. *Charitable Knowledge: Hospital Pupils and Practitioners in Eighteenth-Century London*. Cambridge (England): Cambridge University Press.

*Lesch, John E. 1984. *Science and Medicine in France: The Emergence of Experimental Physiology, 1790-1855*. Cambridge (MA): Harvard University Press.

*Lewontin, Richard C. 1991. *Biology as Ideology: The Doctrine of DNA*. Ontario, Canada: House of Anansi Press Ltd.

*Long, Esmond R. 1928. *A History of Pathology*. Reprint, New York: Dover, 1965.

*Lower, Gerald, and Marty S. Kanarek. 1983. "Conceptual/operational Criteria of Causality: Relevance to Systematic Epidemiologic Theory." *Medical Hypotheses* 11: 217-244.

*MacCallum, W. G. 1920. *A Text-Book of Pathology*, 2nd ed. Philadelphia: W. B. Saunders. books.google.com.

*Mackintosh, John. 1844. *Principles of Pathology and Practice of Medicine*. 4th ed. With notes and additions by Samuel George Morton. Philadelphia: Lindsay and Blakiston.

*Malkin, Harold M. 1993. *Out of the Mist: The Foundation of Modern Pathology and Medicine during the Nineteenth Century*. Berkeley (CA): Vesalius Books.

*Martineau, Harriet. 1875. *The Positive Philosophy of Auguste Comte*, vol 1. 12th ed. Translated and condensed by Harriet Martineau in two volumes. London (England): Trübner. books.google.com.

*Maulitz, Russell C. 1987. *Morbid Appearances: The Anatomy of Pathology in the Early Nineteenth Century*. Cambridge: Cambridge University Press.

*Mayr, Ernst. 1982. *The Growth of Biological Thought: Diversity, Evolution, and Inheritance*. Cambridge: The Belknap Press of Harvard University Press.

*Mazumdar, Pauline M.H., ed. 1989. *Immunology 1930-1980: Essays on the History of Immunology*. Toronto: Wall & Thompson.

*McConnell, Guthrie. 1915. *A Manual of Pathology*. 3rd ed. Philadelphia: W. B. Saunders.

*McMenemey, W. H. 1968. "Cellular Pathology, with Special Reference to the Influence of Virchow's Teachings on Medical Thought and Practice." In Poynter F.N.L., ed. 1968. Medicine and Science in the 1860s, 13-43. London: Wellcome Institute of the History of Medicine.

*McNeely, Ian F., with Lisa Wolverton. 2008. *Reinventing Knowledge: From Alexandria to the Internet*. New York: WW Norton.

Merriam-Webster's Medical Desk Dictionary, rev ed., s.v. "pathology."

*Metchnikoff, Elie. 1968. *Lectures on the Comparative Pathology of Inflammation*. Delivered at the Pasteur Institute in 1891 by Elie Metchnikoff. Translated from the

French by F. A. Starling and E. H. Starling, with a new introduction by Arthur M. Silverstein, The John Hopkins University School of Medicine. New York: Dover Pub.

*Moore, Wendy. 2005. *The Knife Man: Blood, Body Snatching, and the Birth of Modern Surgery*. New York: Broadway Books.

*Morgagni, John Baptist. 1769. *The Seats and Causes of Diseases Investigated by Anatomy, in Five Books, Containing a Great Variety of Dissections, with Remarks*. Translated from Latin by Benjamin Alexander. London: A Millar; and T. Cadell, and Johnson and Payne. Reprint, Birmingham, Alabama: The Classics of Medicine Library, 1983.

*Moulin, Anne-Marie: "Epilogue." 1989. In Mazumdar 1989, 294.

*Mukherjee, Siddhartha. 2011. *The Emperor of All Maladies: A Biography of Cancer*. New York: Scribner.

*------. 2016. *The Gene: An Intimate History*. New York: Scribner.

*Nagel, Jennifer. 2014. *Knowledge: A Very Short Introduction*. Oxford: Oxford University Press.

*Nicholls, A.G. 1927. "The Second Chapter in the History of Pathology." *Canadian Medical Association Journal*. 17: 463-466.

*Oertel, Horst. 1927. *Outlines of Pathology: In Its Historical, Philosophical, and Scientific Foundations. A Guide for Students and Practitioners of Medicine*. Montreal: Renouf Publishing.

*Okasha, Samir. 2002. *Philosophy of Science: A Very Short Introduction*. Oxford: Oxford University Press.

*Ortiz-Hidalgo, Carlos, and Sergio Pina-Oviedo. 2018. "Hematoxylin: Mesoamerica's Gift to Histopathology. *Palo de Campeche* (Logwood Tree), Pirates' Most Desired Treasure, and Irreplaceable Tissue Stain." *International Journal of Surgical Pathology.* 27 (1): 4-14.

*Osler, William. 2009. *The Evolution of Modern Medicine. A Series of Lectures Delivered at Yale University in April 1913.* Foreword by Conrad Fischer. New York: Kaplan Pub.

*Pardue M.L., Gall J.G. 1970. "Chromosomal Localization of Mouse Satellite DNA." *Science* 168 (937): 1356-1358.

*Park, Katharina. 1994. "The Criminal and the Saintly Body: Autopsy and Dissection in Renaissance Italy." *Renaissance Quarterly* 47 (1): 1-33.

*Payne, Joseph Frank. N.d. "Carswell, Robert." *Dictionary of National Biography, 1885-1900,* vol 09. en.wikisource.org.

*Paine, Martyn. 1847. *The Institutes of Medicine.* Reprint, La Vergne, Tennessee: General Books, 2009.

*Pearse, A. G. Everson. 1953. *Histochemistry: Theoretical and Applied.* Boston: Little, Brown and Co.

*Pearson, Karl. 1900. *The Grammar of Science.* 2d ed. London (England): Adam and Charles Black. books.google.com.

*Peng, Albert and A. Bernard Ackerman. 1998. "Neoplasm?" *New Quandary* 4 (1): 41-45.

*Perez-Tamayo, Ruy. 1961. *Mechanisms of Disease: An Introduction to Pathology.* Philadelphia: W.B. Saunders.

*Peven, D.R. and J.D Gruhn. 1985. "The Development of Electron Microscopy." *Archives of Pathology and Laboratory Medicine.* 109: 683-691.

*Porter, Roy. 1999. *The Greatest Benefit to Mankind: A Medical History of Humanity.* New York: W.W. Norton.

*Putschar, Walter G. J. 1973. "Introduction." In Virchow, Rudolph. (1896) 1973. *Post-Mortem Examinations and The Position of Pathology Among Biological Sciences.* With an introduction by Walter G. J. Putschar, i-viii. Reprint, Library of The New York Academy of Medicine. Metuchen (NJ): Scarecrow Reprint Corporation.

*------. 2002. *Blood & Guts: A Short History of Medicine.* New York: W. W. Norton.

*Quinonez, Guillermo. 2002. "Impact of genomic biotechnology on tumour diagnosis in surgical pathology." *Annals of the Royal College of Physicians and Surgeons of Canada.* 35:216-8.

*------. 2010. "The Origin of Basic Science Pathology: An Unrecognized Event in the Medical History Literature." *Canadian Journal of Pathology.* 2 (3): 13-18.

*------ and William W. McLendon. 2011. "The Beginnings of Pathology in America: A Contemporary Analysis of William E. Horner's "A Treatise on Pathological Anatomy."" *Archives of Pathology and Laboratory Medicine.* 135 (12): 1591-1596.

*------ and Laurette Geldenhuys. 2019. "Samuel Clossy's Observations: An Unrecognized Contribution to the Origin of Anatomical Pathology." *Hektoen International Journal of Medical Humanities.* History Essays. Spring.

*Rather, L.J. 1978. *The Genesis of Cancer: A Study in the History of Ideas.* Baltimore: The John Hopkins University Press.

*Reiser, Stanley Joel. 1981. *Medicine and the Reign of Technology.* Cambridge (England): Cambridge University Press.

*Ritchie A. C. 1990. *Boyd's Textbook of Pathology*, vol. 1. 9th ed. Philadelphia: Lea & Febiger.

*Robb-Smith, A. H. T. 1970. "The Functional Significance of Connective Tissue." In Florey 1970, 451.

*Robbins, Stanley L., and Ramzi S. Cotran. 1979. *Pathologic Basis of Disease.* 2d ed. Philadelphia: W. B. Sanders.

*Rodin, Alvin E. 1973. *The Influence of Matthew Baillie's Morbid Anatomy: Biography, Evaluation and Reprint.* Springfield (IL): Charles C Thomas.

*------. *Oslerian Pathology: An Assessment and Annotated Atlas of Museum Specimens.* 1981. Lawrence (KS): Coronado Press.

*Rokitansky, Carl. 1854. *A Manual of Pathological Anatomy*, vol 1. Translated by William Edward Swaine. London: Sydenham Society.

*Rosenberg, Charles E. 1987. *The Cholera Years: The United States in 1832, 1849, and 1866.* Chicago: The University of Chicago Press.

*Rothschuh, Karl E. 1973. *History of Physiology.* Translated and edited by Guenter B. Risse. New York: Robert E. Krieger Pub.

*Rous, Peyton. 1911. "A Sarcoma of the Fowl Transmissible by an Agent Separable from the Tumor Cells." *Journal of Experimental Medicine.* 13 (4): 397-411.

*Rymer, James. 1775. *Introduction to the Study of Pathology on a Natural Plan: Containing an Essay on Fevers.* London: Donaldson.

*Satyarup, D., Kumar, M., Dalai, R.P., Mohanty, S., and Rathor, K.R. 2020. "Theories of Disease Causation: An Overview." *Indian Journal of Forensic Medicine & Toxicology.* 14 (4): 8075-8079.

*Scarani, Paoli, Gian Paolo Salvioli, and Vincenzo Eusebi. 1994. "Marcello Malpighi (1628-1694). A Founding Father of Modern Anatomic Pathology." *American Journal of Surgical Pathology.* 18: 741-746.

*Shapin, Steven, and Simon Schaffer. 1985. *Leviathan and the Air-Pump: Hobbes, Boyle, and the Experimental Life.* Princeton (NJ): Princeton University Press.

*Sherrington, Charles. 1946. *The Endeavour of Jean Fernel: With a List of the Editions of his Writings.* Cambridge: Cambridge University Press.

*Shope, Richard E. 1932. "Transmissible Tumor-like Condition in Rabbits." *Journal of Experimental Medicine.* 56 (6): 793-802.

*Sigerist, Henry E. 1932. *Man and Medicine: An Introduction to Medical Knowledge.* Translated by Margaret Galt Boise and introduction by William H. Welch. New York: WW Norton.

*Singer, Charles, and E. Ashworth Underwood. 1962. *A Short History of Medicine.* 2d ed. Oxford: Oxford University Press.

*Snyder, Laura J. 2015. *Eye of the Beholder: Johannes Vermeer, Antoni van Leeuwenhoek, and the Reinvention of Seeing.* New York: W. W. Norton.

*Sokal, Robert R. 1974. "Classification: Purposes, Principles, Progress, Prospects." *Science*. 185 (4157): 1115-1123. Science.org/toc/science/185(4157).

*Sosa, Ernest. 2017. *Epistemology*. Princeton (NJ): Princeton University Press.

*Southern E.M. 1975. "Detection of Specific Sequences Among DNA Fragments Separated by Gel Electrophoresis." *Journal of Molecular Biology*. 98 (3): 503-517.

*Spear, Caitlin, Maggie Reilly, and Stuart W McDonald. 2018. "Matthew Baillie's Specimens and Engravings." *Clinical Anatomy*. 31: 622-631.

*Stengel, Alfred. 1900. *A Text-Book of Pathology*. 3rd ed. Philadelphia: W. B. Saunders.

*Sudhoff, Karl. 1926. *Essays in the History of Medicine*. Translated by various hands and edited, with foreword and biographical sketch, by Fielding H. Garrison. New York: Medical Life Press.

*Temkin, Owsei. 1977. *The Double Face of Janus: and Other Essays in the History of Medicine*. Baltimore: The Johns Hopkins University Press.

**The Beautiful Brain: The Drawings of Santiago Ramón y Cajal*. 2017. Edited and commentaries by Larry W. Swanson, Eric A. Newman, Alfonso Araque, Janet M. Dubinsky, Lyndel King, and Eric Himmel. New York: Abrams.

**The New Lexicon Webster's Encyclopedic Dictionary of the English Language, Canadian Edition*, s.v. "technique."

*Trombley, Stephen. 2011. *A History of Western Thought*. London (England): Atlantic Books.

*Vernon-Roberts, B. 1972. *The Macrophage*. Cambridge: Cambridge University Press.

*Vesalius, *The Epitome of Andreas Vesalius*. 1944. Translated from the latin with preface and introduction by L.R. Lind, with anatomical notes by C.W. Asling, and foreword by L. Clendening. New York: Macmillan Co.

*Vincent M.D. 1987. "The Definition of a Neoplasm." *Medical Hypothesis*. 24: 151-160.

*Virchow, Rudolph. (1860) 1978. *Cellular Pathology as Based upon Physiological and Pathological Histology*. 2nd ed. Translated by Frank Chance. London: John Churchill, New Burlington Street. Reprint, Birmingham, Alabama: The Classics of Medicine Library.

*Vollmer E., and Goldmann T. 2011. "Pathology on the Edge of Interdisciplinarity. A Historical Epitome." *Romanian Journal of Morphology and Embryology*. 52 (1 Suppl): 223-230.

*Wagner, Ernst. 1876. *A Manual of General Pathology. For the Use of Students and Practitioners of Medicine*. 6th ed. New York: William Wood & Co.

*Waksman, Byron H. 1989. "Cell Mediated Immunity." In Mazumdar 1989, 148-149, 149-154.

*Weakley, B.S. 1981. *A Beginner's Handbook in Biological Transmission Electron Microscopy*. 2nd. ed. Great Britain: Churchill Livingstone.

*Welch, William H. (1897) 1937. "Adaptation in Pathological Processes." *Transactions of the Congress of American Physicians and Surgeons*. 4: 284-310. Reprint with an introduction by Simon Flexner. Baltimore: The Johns Hopkins Press, 1937.

*Westerhoff, Jan. 2011. *Reality: A Very Short Introduction*. Oxford: Oxford University Press.

*Wick, Mark R. 2012. "Histochemistry as a Tool in Morphological Analysis: A Historical Review." *Annals of Diagnostic Pathology*. 16: 71-78.

*Willis, R.A. 1967. *Pathology of Tumours*. 4rd ed. London (England): Butterworhts.

*Wright, G. Pauling. 1958. *An Introduction to Pathology*. 3rd ed. London (England): Longmans Green.

*Wright Jr., James R. 2012. "Albert C. Broders' Paradigm Shifts Involving the Prognostication and Definition of Cancer." *Archives of Pathology and Laboratory Medicine*. 136: 1437-1446.

*Zhang, Fang F., D.C. Michaels, B. Mathema, et al. 2004. "Evolution of Epidemiologic Methods and Concepts in Selected Textbooks of the 20th Century." *Sozial-und Praventivmedicin*. 49 (2): 97-104. DOI 10.1007/s00038-004-3117-8.

*Ziegler, Ernst. 1883. *A Text-Book of General Pathology and Pathogenesis*. 2nd ed. Translated by Donald Macalister. New York: William Wood & Co.